The Complete Tefal Dual Zone Air Fryer Cookbook for Beginners

1200 Days Easy, Flavorful and Effortless Air Fryer Recipes Helping You Master the Dual Zone Air Fryer

Vivian M. Gibson

All Rights Reserved.

The content contained within this book may not be reproduced, duplicated, or transmitted without direct written permission from the author or the publisher. Under no circumstances will any blame or legal responsibility be held against the publisher, or author, for any damages, reparation, or monetary loss due to the information contained within this book, either directly or indirectly.

Legal Notice: This book is copyright protected. It is only for personal use. You cannot amend, distribute, sell, use, quote or paraphrase any part, or the content within this book, without the consent of the author or publisher.

Disclaimer Notice:

Please note the information contained within this document is for educational and entertainment purposes only. All effort has been executed to present accurate, up to date, reliable, complete information. No warranties of any kind are declared or implied. Readers acknowledge that the author is not engaged in the rendering of legal, financial, medical, or professional advice. The content within this book has been derived from various sources. Please consult a licensed professional before attempting any techniques outlined in this book. By reading this document, the reader agrees that under no circumstances is the author responsible for any losses, direct or indirect, that are incurred as a result of the use of the information contained within this document, including, but not limited to, errors, omissions, or inaccuracies.

CONTENTS

MEASUREMENT CONVERSIONS 12

Breakfast Recipes 14

Sweet Potato Sausage Hash 14

Crispy Hash Browns 14

Breakfast Sammies 15

Bacon Cinnamon Rolls 15

Cinnamon Toast 16

Mushroom-and-tomato Stuffed Hash Browns 16

Air Fried Bacon And Eggs 16

Quiche Breakfast Peppers 17

Sausage With Eggs 17

Cheddar-ham-corn Muffins 17

Blueberry Muffins 18

Cinnamon-raisin Bagels Everything Bagels 18

Perfect Cinnamon Toast 19

Yellow Potatoes With Eggs 19

Mozzarella Bacon Calzones 19

Blueberry Coffee Cake And Maple Sausage Patties 20

Quick And Easy Blueberry Muffins 20

Cheesy Baked Eggs 21

Wholemeal Blueberry Muffins 21

Lemon-blueberry Muffins 21

Mexican Breakfast Pepper Rings 22

Sweet Potato Hash 22

Roasted Oranges 22

Sausage And Cheese Balls 22

Baked Egg And Mushroom Cups 22

French Toast Sticks 23

Homemade Toaster Pastries 23

Cheesy Scrambled Eggs And Egg And Bacon Muffins 24

anadian Bacon Muffin Sandwiches And All-in-one Toast 24

Pumpkin French Toast Casserole With Sweet And Spicy Twisted Bacon 25

Egg And Avocado In The Tefal 25

Eggs In Avocado Cups 26

Vanilla Strawberry Doughnuts 26

Turkey Ham Muffins 26

Air Fried Sausage 27

Sausage And Egg Breakfast Burrito 27

Bagels 27

Breakfast Calzone And Western Frittata 28

Bacon & Spinach Cups 28

Banana Bread 29

Snacks And Appetizers Recipes 29

Croquettes 29

Blueberries Muffins 30

Buffalo Wings Honey-garlic Wings 30

Tangy Fried Pickle Spears 31

Goat Cheese And Garlic Crostini & Sweet Bacon Potato Crunchies 31

Waffle Fries 31

Cheese Stuffed Mushrooms 32

Chicken Tenders 32

Crispy Plantain Chips 32

Cauliflower Gnocchi 33

Healthy Spinach Balls 33

Beef Skewers 33

Pepperoni Pizza Dip 34

Ravioli 34

Shrimp Pirogues 34

Healthy Chickpea Fritters 35

Fried Pickles 35

Beefy Swiss Pastry 35

Spinach Patties 36

Crispy Popcorn Shrimp 36

Five-ingredient Falafel With Garlic-yoghurt Sauce 36

Vegetables And Sides Recipes 37

Garlic-rosemary Brussels Sprouts 37

Stuffed Tomatoes 37

Rosemary Asparagus & Potatoes 37

Bacon Potato Patties 38

Jerk Tofu With Roasted Cabbage 38

Veggie Burgers With "fried" Onion Rings 39

Potatoes & Beans 39

Garlic Potato Wedges In Air Fryer 40

Bacon Wrapped Corn Cob 40

Fried Avocado Tacos 40

Acorn Squash Slices 41

Fried Olives 41

Stuffed Sweet Potatoes 41

Air Fryer Vegetables 42

Potato And Parsnip Latkes With Baked Apples 42

Green Tomato Stacks 43

Chickpea Fritters 43

Pepper Poppers 44

Fresh Mix Veggies In Air Fryer 44

Fried Artichoke Hearts 44

Buffalo Bites 45

Beef, Pork, And Lamb Recipes 45

Bo Luc Lac 45

Steak Fajitas With Onions And Peppers 46

Easy Breaded Pork Chops 46

Mozzarella Stuffed Beef And Pork Meatballs 46

Sausage Meatballs 47

Garlic Butter Steaks 47

Steak And Mashed Creamy Potatoes 47

Tasty Pork Skewers 48

Air Fryer Meatloaves 48

Sausage And Pork Meatballs 48

Tomahawk Steak 49

Simple Beef Sirloin Roast 49

Pork Chops With Apples 49

Five-spice Pork Belly 50

Cheeseburgers With Barbecue Potato Chips 50

Tender Pork Chops 51

Barbecue Ribs With Roasted Green Beans And Shallots 51

Seasoned Flank Steak 51

Tasty Lamb Patties 52

Italian Sausages With Peppers And Teriyaki Rump Steak With Broccoli 52

Roast Souvlaki-style Pork With Lemon-feta Baby Potatoes 53

Paprika Pork Chops 53

Beef And Bean Taquitos With Mexican Rice 54

Turkey And Beef Meatballs 54

Panko Crusted Calf's Liver Strips 55

Bacon-wrapped Hot Dogs With Mayo-ketchup Sauce 55

Meatloaf 55

Air Fryer Chicken-fried Steak 56

Balsamic Steak Tips With Roasted Asparagus And Mushroom Medley 56

Cinnamon-beef Kofta 56

Fish And Seafood Recipes 57

Cod With Jalapeño 57

Salmon With Cauliflower 57

Stuffed Mushrooms With Crab 57

Honey Sriracha Mahi Mahi 57

Salmon Patties 58

Tilapia Sandwiches With Tartar Sauce 58

Orange-mustard Glazed Salmon And Cucumber And Salmon Salad 59

Country Prawns 59

Bacon-wrapped Shrimp 60

Honey Teriyaki Tilapia 60

Tuna With Herbs 60

Smoked Salmon 61

Tuna Steaks 61

Classic Fish Sticks With Tartar Sauce 61

Salmon With Fennel Salad 62

Crumb-topped Sole 62

Frozen Breaded Fish Fillet 62

Tuna Patties With Spicy Sriracha Sauce Coconut Prawns 63

Roasted Salmon And Parmesan Asparagus 63

Herb Tuna Patties 64

Salmon Nuggets 64

Brown Sugar Garlic Salmon 64

Bacon Halibut Steak 65

Pretzel-crusted Catfish 65

Sole And Cauliflower Fritters And Prawn Bake 65

Crusted Cod 66

Lemony Prawns And Courgette 66

Sesame Honey Salmon 66

Foil Packet Salmon 67

Cajun Catfish Cakes With Cheese 67

Italian Baked Cod 67

Roasted Halibut Steaks With Parsley 68

Scallops 68

Oyster Po'boy 68

Broiled Crab Cakes With Hush Puppies 69

Tuna Patties 69

Prawns Curry 70

Perfect Parmesan Salmon 70

Shrimp With Lemon And Pepper 70

Breaded Scallops 71

Poultry Recipes 71

Crispy Dill Chicken Strips 71

Garlic Dill Wings 71

Chicken Potatoes 72

Chicken Parmesan 72

Lemon Thyme Roasted Chicken 72

Coriander Lime Chicken Thighs 73

Buffalo Chicken 73

Balsamic Duck Breast 73

General Tso's Chicken 74

Almond Chicken 74

Chicken Drumettes 75

Cheddar-stuffed Chicken 75

Wings With Corn On Cob 75

Turkey Meatloaf With Veggie Medley 76

Bell Pepper Stuffed Chicken Roll-ups 76

Turkey And Cranberry Quesadillas 76

Harissa-rubbed Chicken 77

Herbed Turkey Breast With Simple Dijon Sauce 77

Chicken And Vegetable Fajitas 77

Spice-rubbed Chicken Pieces 78

Bang-bang Chicken 78

Sweet And Spicy Carrots With Chicken Thighs 78

Chicken Legs With Leeks 79

Chicken And Potatoes 79

Bbq Cheddar-stuffed Chicken Breasts 79

Italian Chicken & Potatoes 80

Yummy Chicken Breasts 80

Broccoli Cheese Chicken 80

Orange Chicken With Roasted Snap Peas And Scallions 81

Thai Curry Chicken Kabobs 81

Chili Chicken Wings 82

Air-fried Turkey Breast With Roasted Green Bean Casserole 82

Chicken Wings With Piri Piri Sauce 83

Chicken & Veggies 83

Bruschetta Chicken 83

Chicken With Bacon And Tomato & Bacon-wrapped Stuffed Chicken Breasts 84

Chicken Fajitas With Street Corn 84

Fajita Chicken Strips & Barbecued Chicken With Creamy Coleslaw 85

Chipotle Drumsticks 85

Spicy Chicken Sandwiches With "fried" Pickles 86

Marinated Chicken Legs 86

Honey Butter Chicken 87

Desserts Recipes 87

Soft Pecan Brownies 87

Stuffed Apples 87

Chocolate Muffins 88

Mini Peanut Butter Tarts 88

Berry Crumble And Coconut-custard Pie 89

Quickie Cinnamon Sugar Pork Rinds 89

Mini Strawberry And Cream Pies 89

Olive Oil Cake & Old-fashioned Fudge Pie 90

Lime Bars 90

Healthy Semolina Pudding 90

Moist Chocolate Espresso Muffins 91

Fluffy Layered Peanut Butter Cheesecake Brownies 91

Lemony Sweet Twists 91

Fudge Brownies 92

Cinnamon Bread Twists 92

Easy Mini Chocolate Chip Pan Cookie 92

Apple Nutmeg Flautas 93

Walnuts Fritters 93

Chocolate Chip Pecan Biscotti 94

Fruity Blackberry Crisp 94

Cake In The Air Fryer 94

Apple Hand Pies 95

Victoria Sponge Cake 95

Monkey Bread 96

Lemon Sugar Cookie Bars Monster Sugar Cookie Bars 96

Spiced Apple Cake 97

Biscuit Doughnuts 97

Apple Crumble 97

Apple Wedges With Apricots And Coconut Mixed Berry Crisp 98

Honeyed, Roasted Apples With Walnuts & Rhubarb And Strawberry Crumble 98

Simple Pineapple Sticks And Crispy Pineapple Rings 99

Apple Pie Rolls 99

RECIPES INDEX 100

MEASUREMENT CONVERSIONS

BASIC KITCHEN CONVERSIONS & EQUIVALENTS

DRY MEASUREMENTS CONVERSION CHART

3 TEASPOONS = 1 TABLESPOON = 1/16 CUP
6 TEASPOONS = 2 TABLESPOONS = 1/8 CUP
12 TEASPOONS = 4 TABLESPOONS = 1/4 CUP
24 TEASPOONS = 8 TABLESPOONS = 1/2 CUP
36 TEASPOONS = 12 TABLESPOONS = 3/4 CUP
48 TEASPOONS = 16 TABLESPOONS = 1 CUP

METRIC TO US COOKING CONVER-SIONS

OVEN TEMPERATURES

120 °C = 250 °F
160 °C = 320 °F
180 °C = 350 °F
205 °C = 400 °F
220 °C = 425 °F

LIQUID MEASUREMENTS CONVERSION CHART

8 FLUID OUNCES = 1 CUP = 1/2 PINT = 1/4 QUART
16 FLUID OUNCES = 2 CUPS = 1 PINT = 1/2 QUART
32 FLUID OUNCES = 4 CUPS = 2 PINTS = 1 QUART
1/4 GALLON
128 FLUID OUNCES = 16 CUPS = 8 PINTS = 4 QUARTS = 1 GALLON

BAKING IN GRAMS

1 CUP FLOUR = 140 GRAMS
1 CUP SUGAR = 150 GRAMS
1 CUP POWDERED SUGAR=160 GRAMS
1 CUP HEAVY CREAM = 235 GRAMS

VOLUME

1 MILLILITER=1/5 TEASPOON
5 ML = 1 TEASPOON
15 ML = 1 TABLESPOON
240 ML = 1 CUP OR 8 FLUID OUNCES
1 LITER=34 FL. OUNCES

WEIGHT

1 GRAM = 035 OUNCES
100 GRAMS=3.5 OUNCES
500 GRAMS = 1.1 POUNDS
1 KILOGRAM=35 OUNCES

US TO METRIC COOKING CONVERSIONS

1/5 TSP = 1 ML
1 TSP=5 ML
1 TBSP = 15 ML
1 FL OUNCE = 30 ML
1 CUP=237 ML
1 PINT (2 CUPS) = 473 ML
1 QUART (4 CUPS)=.95 LITER
1GALLON (16 CUPS)=3.8LITERS
1 OZ=28 GRAMS
1 POUND = 454 GRAMS

BUTTER

1 CUP BUTTER=2 STICKS = 8 OUNCES = 230 GRAMS=8 TABLESPOONS

WHAT DOES 1 CUP EQUAL

1 CUP = 8 FLUID OUNCES
1 CUP = 16 TABLESPOONS
1 CUP = 48 TEASPOONS
1 CUP = 1/2 PINT
1 CUP = 1/4 QUART
1 CUP = 1/16 GALLON
1 CUP = 240 ML

BAKING PAN CONVERSIONS

1 CUP ALL-PURPOSE FLOUR=4.5 OZ
1 CUP ROLLED OATS = 3 OZ 1 LARGE EGG = 1.7 OZ
1 CUP BUTTER=8OZ 1 CUP MILK = 8 OZ
1 CUP HEAVY CREAM = 8.4 OZ
1 CUP GRANULATED SUGAR=7.1 OZ
1 CUP PACKED BROWN SUGAR = 7.75 OZ
1 CUP VEGETABLE OIL = 7.7 OZ
1 CUP UNSIFTED POWDERED SUGAR = 4.4 OZ

BAKING PAN CONVERSIONS

9-INCH ROUND CAKE PAN= 12 CUPS
10-INCH TUBE PAN =16 CUPS
11-INCH BUNDT PAN = 12 CUPS
9-INCH SPRINGFORM PAN = 10 CUPS
9 X 5 INCH LOAF PAN=8 CUPS
9-INCH SQUARE PAN=8 CUPS

Breakfast Recipes

Sweet Potato Sausage Hash

Servings: 4
Cooking Time: 20 Minutes
Ingredients:
- 1½ pounds sweet potato, peeled and diced into ½-inch pieces
- 1 tablespoon minced garlic
- 1 teaspoon kosher salt plus more, as desired
- Ground black pepper, as desired
- 2 tablespoons canola oil
- 1 tablespoon dried sage
- 1-pound uncooked mild ground breakfast sausage
- ½ large onion, peeled and diced
- ½ teaspoon ground cinnamon
- 1 teaspoon chili powder
- 4 large eggs, poached or fried (optional)

Directions:
1. Toss the sweet potatoes with the garlic, salt, pepper, and canola oil in a mixing bowl.
2. Install the crisper plate in the zone 1 drawer, fill it with the sweet potato mixture, and insert the drawer in the unit.
3. Place the ground sausage in the zone 2 drawer (without the crisper plate) and place it in the unit.
4. Select zone 1, then AIR FRY, and set the temperature to 400 degrees F/ 200 degrees C with a 30-minute timer.
5. Select zone 2, then ROAST, then set the temperature to 400 degrees F/ 200 degrees C with a 20-minute timer. SYNC is the option to choose. To begin cooking, press the START/STOP button.
6. When the zone 1 and zone 2 times have reached 10 minutes, press START/STOP and remove the drawers from the unit. Shake each for 10 seconds.
7. Half of the sage should be added to the zone 1 drawer.
8. Add the onion to the zone 2 drawer and mix to incorporate. To continue cooking, press START/STOP and reinsert the drawers.
9. Remove both drawers from the unit once the cooking is finished and add the potatoes to the sausage mixture. Mix in the cinnamon, sage, chili powder, and salt until thoroughly combined.
10. When the hash is done, stir it and serve it right away with a poached or fried egg on top, if desired.

Nutrition:
- (Per serving) Calories 491 | Fat 19.5g | Sodium 736mg | Carbs 51g | Fiber 8g | Sugar 2g | Protein 26.3

Crispy Hash Browns

Servings: 4
Cooking Time: 13 Minutes.
Ingredients:
- 3 russet potatoes
- ¼ cup chopped green peppers
- ¼ cup chopped red peppers
- ¼ cup chopped onions
- 2 garlic cloves chopped
- 1 teaspoon paprika
- Salt and black pepper, to taste
- 2 teaspoons olive oil

Directions:
1. Peel and grate all the potatoes with the help of a cheese grater.
2. Add potato shreds to a bowl filled with cold water and leave it soaked for 25 minutes.
3. Drain the water and place the potato shreds on a plate lined with a paper towel.
4. Transfer the shreds to a dry bowl and add olive oil, paprika, garlic, and black pepper.
5. Make four flat patties out of the potato mixture and place two into each of the crisper plate.
6. Return the crisper plate to the Tefal Dual Zone Air Fryer.
7. Choose the Air Fry mode for Zone 1 and set the temperature to 390 degrees F and set the time to 13 minutes.
8. Select the "MATCH" button to copy the settings for Zone 2.
9. Initiate cooking by pressing the START/STOP button.
10. Flip the potato hash browns once cooked halfway through, then resume cooking.
11. Once done, serve warm.

Nutrition:
- (Per serving) Calories 190 | Fat 18g | Sodium 150mg | Carbs 0.6g | Fiber 0.4g | Sugar 0.4g | Protein 7.2g

Breakfast Sammies

Servings: 5
Cooking Time: 20 Minutes
Ingredients:
- Biscuits:
- 6 large egg whites
- 475 ml blanched almond flour, plus more if needed
- 1½ teaspoons baking powder
- ½ teaspoon fine sea salt
- 60 ml (½ stick) very cold unsalted butter (or lard for dairy-free), cut into ¼-inch pieces
- Eggs:
- 5 large eggs
- ½ teaspoon fine sea salt
- ¼ teaspoon ground black pepper
- 5 (30 g) slices Cheddar cheese (omit for dairy-free)
- 10 thin slices ham

Directions:
1. Spray the two air fryer drawers with avocado oil. Preheat the air fryer to 176°C. Grease two pie pans or two baking pans that will fit inside your air fryer. 2. Make the biscuits: In a medium-sized bowl, whip the egg whites with a hand mixer until very stiff. Set aside. 3. In a separate medium-sized bowl, stir together the almond flour, baking powder, and salt until well combined. Cut in the butter. Gently fold the flour mixture into the egg whites with a rubber spatula. If the dough is too wet to form into mounds, add a few tablespoons of almond flour until the dough holds together well. 4. Using a large spoon, divide the dough into 5 equal portions and drop them about 1 inch apart on one of the greased pie pans. Place the pan in the two air fryer drawers and bake for 11 to 14 minutes, until the biscuits are golden brown. Remove from the air fryer and set aside to cool. 5. Make the eggs: Set the air fryer to 192°C. Crack the eggs into the remaining greased pie pan and sprinkle with the salt and pepper. Place the eggs in the air fryer to bake for 5 minutes, or until they are cooked to your liking. 6. Open the air fryer and top each egg yolk with a slice of cheese. Bake for another minute, or until the cheese is melted. 7. Once the biscuits are cool, slice them in half lengthwise. Place 1 cooked egg topped with cheese and 2 slices of ham in each biscuit. 8. Store leftover biscuits, eggs, and ham in separate airtight containers in the fridge for up to 3 days. Reheat the biscuits and eggs on a baking sheet in a preheated 176°C air fryer for 5 minutes, or until warmed through.

Bacon Cinnamon Rolls

Servings: 8
Cooking Time: 10 Minutes
Ingredients:
- 8 bacon strips
- 180ml bourbon
- 1 tube (310g) refrigerated cinnamon rolls with icing
- 55g chopped pecans
- 2 tablespoons maple syrup

Directions:
1. In a small bowl, combine the bacon and the bourbon. Refrigerate overnight after sealing. Remove the bacon and pat it dry; toss out the bourbon.
2. Cook bacon in batches in a large frying pan over medium heat until nearly crisp but still flexible. Remove to a plate lined with paper towels to drain.
3. Separate the dough into 8 rolls and set aside the frosting packet. Spiral rolls should be unrolled into long strips.
4. Place 1 bacon strip on each dough strip, cut as necessary, and reroll to form a spiral. To seal the ends, pinch them together.
5. Press your chosen zone - "Zone 1" or "Zone 2" and then rotate the knob to select "Air Fry".
6. Set the temperature to 175 degrees C, and then set the time for 5 minutes to preheat.
7. After preheating, spray the Air-Fryer basket of each zone with cooking spray, line them with parchment paper, and place rolls.
8. Slide the basket into the Air Fryer and set the time for 5 minutes.
9. Turn the rolls over and cook for another 4 minutes, or until golden brown.
10. Meanwhile, combine the pecans and maple syrup in a mixing bowl. In a separate bowl, combine the contents of the icing packet.
11. Heat the remaining bacon drippings in the same frying pan over medium heat. Cook, stirring regularly until the pecan mixture is gently browned, about 2-3 minutes.
12. After cooking time is completed, transfer them onto serving plates and drizzle half the icing over warm cinnamon rolls; top with half the pecans.

Cinnamon Toast

Servings: 6
Cooking Time: 5 Minutes
Ingredients:
- 12 slices bread
- 115g butter, at room temperature
- 100g white sugar
- 1½ teaspoons ground cinnamon
- 1½ teaspoons pure vanilla extract
- 1 pinch of salt

Directions:
1. Softened butter is mashed with a fork or the back of a spoon, and then sugar, cinnamon, vanilla, and salt are added.
2. Stir everything together thoroughly.
3. Spread one-sixth of the mixture onto each slice of bread, covering the entire surface.
4. Press your chosen zone - "Zone 1" or "Zone 2" and then rotate the knob to select "Air Fryer".
5. Set the temperature to 200 degrees C, and then set the time for 3 minutes to preheat.
6. After preheating, arrange bread into the basket of each zone.
7. Slide the basket into the Air Fryer and set the time for 5 minutes.
8. After cooking time is completed, remove both baskets from Air Fryer.
9. Cut bread slices diagonally and serve.

Mushroom-and-tomato Stuffed Hash Browns

Servings: 4
Cooking Time: 20 Minutes
Ingredients:
- Olive oil cooking spray
- 1 tablespoon plus 2 teaspoons olive oil, divided
- 110 g baby mushrooms, diced
- 1 spring onion, white parts and green parts, diced
- 1 garlic clove, minced
- 475 ml shredded potatoes
- ½ teaspoon salt
- ¼ teaspoon black pepper
- 1 plum tomato, diced
- 120 ml shredded mozzarella

Directions:
1. Lightly coat the inside of a 6-inch cake pan with olive oil cooking spray. In a small skillet, heat 2 teaspoons olive oil over medium heat. Add the mushrooms, spring onion, and garlic, and cook for 4 to 5 minutes, or until they have softened and are beginning to show some color.
2. Remove from heat. Meanwhile, in a large bowl, combine the potatoes, salt, pepper, and the remaining tablespoon olive oil. Toss until all potatoes are well coated. Pour half of the potatoes into the bottom of the cake pan.
3. Top with the mushroom mixture, tomato, and mozzarella. Spread the remaining potatoes over the top. Place the cake pan into the zone 1 drawer.
4. Select Bake button and adjust temperature to 190°C, set time to 12 to 15 minutes and press Start. Until the top is golden brown, remove from the air fryer and allow to cool for 5 minutes before slicing and serving.

Air Fried Bacon And Eggs

Servings: 1
Cooking Time: 10 Minutes
Ingredients:
- 2 eggs
- 2 slices bacon

Directions:
1. Grease a ramekin using cooking spray.
2. Install the crisper plate in the zone 1 drawer and place the bacon inside it. Insert the drawer into the unit.
3. Crack the eggs and add them to the greased ramekin.
4. Install the crisper plate in the zone 2 drawer and place the ramekin inside it. Insert the drawer into the unit.
5. Select zone 1 to AIR FRY for 9–11 minutes at 400 degrees F/ 200 degrees C. Select zone 2 to AIR FRY for 8–9 minutes at 350 degrees F/ 175 degrees C. Press SYNC.
6. Press START/STOP to begin cooking.
7. Enjoy!

Nutrition:
- (Per serving) Calories 331 | Fat 24.5g | Sodium 1001mg | Carbs 1.2g | Fiber 0g | Sugar 0.7g | Protein 25.3g

Quiche Breakfast Peppers

Servings: 4
Cooking Time: 15 Minutes
Ingredients:
- 4 eggs
- ½ tsp garlic powder
- 112g mozzarella cheese, shredded
- 125g ricotta cheese
- 2 bell peppers, cut in half & remove seeds
- 7½g baby spinach, chopped
- 22g parmesan cheese, grated
- ¼ tsp dried parsley

Directions:
1. In a bowl, whisk eggs, ricotta cheese, garlic powder, parsley, cheese, and spinach.
2. Pour the egg mixture into each bell pepper half and top with mozzarella cheese.
3. Insert a crisper plate in the Tefal air fryer baskets.
4. Place bell peppers in both the baskets.
5. Select zone 1 then select "air fry" mode and set the temperature to 355 degrees F for 15 minutes. Press "match" to match zone 2 settings to zone 1. Press "start/stop" to begin.

Nutrition:
- (Per serving) Calories 136 | Fat 7.6g |Sodium 125mg | Carbs 6.9g | Fiber 0.9g | Sugar 3.5g | Protein 10.8g

Sausage With Eggs

Servings:2
Cooking Time:13
Ingredients:
- 4 sausage links, raw and uncooked
- 4 eggs, uncooked
- 1 tablespoon of green onion
- 2 tablespoons of chopped tomatoes
- Salt and black pepper, to taste
- 2 tablespoons of milk, dairy
- Oil spray, for greasing

Directions:
1. Take a bowl and whisk eggs in it.
2. Then pour milk, and add onions and tomatoes.
3. Whisk it all well.
4. Now season it with salt and black pepper.
5. Take one cake pan, that fit inside the air fryer and grease it with oil spray.
6. Pour the omelet in the greased cake pans.
7. Put the cake pan inside zone 1 air fryer basket of Tefale 2-Basket Air Fryer.
8. Now place the sausage link into the zone 2 basket.
9. Select bake for zone 1 basket and set the timer to 8-10 minutes at 300 degrees F.
10. For the zone 2 basket, select the AIR FRY button and set the timer to 12 minutes at 390 degrees.
11. Once the cooking cycle completes, serve by transferring it to plates.
12. Chop the sausage or cut it in round and then mix it with omelet.
13. Enjoy hot as a delicious breakfast.

Nutrition:
- (Per serving) Calories 240 | Fat 18.4g| Sodium 396mg | Carbs 2.8g | Fiber0.2g | Sugar 2g | Protein 15.6g

Cheddar-ham-corn Muffins

Servings: 8 Muffins
Cooking Time: 6 To 8 Minutes
Ingredients:
- 180 ml cornmeal/polenta
- 60 ml flour
- 1½ teaspoons baking powder
- ¼ teaspoon salt
- 1 egg, beaten
- 2 tablespoons rapeseed oil
- 120 ml milk
- 120 ml shredded sharp Cheddar cheese
- 120 ml diced ham
- 8 foil muffin cups, liners removed and sprayed with cooking spray

Directions:
1. Preheat the air fryer to 200°C.
2. In a medium bowl, stir together the cornmeal, flour, baking powder, and salt.
3. Add egg, oil, and milk to dry ingredients and mix well.
4. Stir in shredded cheese and diced ham.
5. Divide batter among the muffin cups.
6. Place filled muffin cups in two air fryer drawers and bake for 5 minutes.
7. Reduce temperature to 166°C and bake for 1 to 2 minutes or until toothpick inserted in center of muffin comes out clean.

Blueberry Muffins

Servings: 12
Cooking Time: 12 Minutes
Ingredients:
- 2 egg, beaten
- 2 ripe bananas, peeled and mashed
- 220g almond flour
- 4 tablespoons granulated sugar
- 1 teaspoon baking powder
- 2 tablespoons coconut oil, melted
- 80g maple syrup
- 2 teaspoons apple cider vinegar
- 2 teaspoons vanilla extract
- 2 teaspoons lemon zest, grated
- Pinch of ground cinnamon
- 150g fresh blueberries

Directions:
1. In a large bowl, add all the ingredients except blueberries and mix until well combined.
2. Gently fold in the blueberries.
3. Grease 2 muffin tins.
4. Place the mixture into prepared muffin cups about ¾ full.
5. Press your chosen zone - "Zone 1" or "Zone 2" and then rotate the knob to select "Bake".
6. Set the temperature to 190 degrees C and then set the time for 5 minutes to preheat.
7. After preheating, arrange 1 muffin tin into the basket of each zone.
8. Slide the basket into the Air Fryer and set the time for 12 minutes.
9. After cooking time is completed, remove the muffin tins from Air Fryer.
10. Place both tins onto a wire rack to cool for 10 minutes.
11. Invert the blueberry muffins onto the wire rack to cool completely before serving.

Cinnamon-raisin Bagels Everything Bagels

Servings: 4
Cooking Time: 14 Minutes
Ingredients:
- FOR THE BAGEL DOUGH
- 1 cup all-purpose flour, plus more for dusting
- 2 teaspoons baking powder
- 1 teaspoon kosher salt
- 1 cup reduced-fat plain Greek yogurt
- FOR THE CINNAMON-RAISIN BAGELS
- ¼ cup raisins
- ½ teaspoon ground cinnamon
- FOR THE EVERYTHING BAGELS
- ¼ teaspoon poppy seeds
- ¼ teaspoon sesame seeds
- ¼ teaspoon dried minced garlic
- ¼ teaspoon dried minced onion
- FOR THE EGG WASH
- 1 large egg
- 1 tablespoon water

Directions:
1. To prep the bagels: In a large bowl, combine the flour, baking powder, and salt. Stir in the yogurt to form a soft dough. Turn the dough out onto a lightly floured surface and knead five to six times, until it is smooth and elastic. Divide the dough in half.
2. Knead the raisins and cinnamon into one dough half. Leave the other dough half plain.
3. Divide both portions of dough in half to form a total of 4 balls of dough (2 cinnamon-raisin and 2 plain). Roll each ball of dough into a rope about 8 inches long. Shape each rope into a ring and pinch the ends to seal.
4. To prep the everything bagels: In a small bowl, mix together the poppy seeds, sesame seeds, garlic, and onion.
5. To prep the egg wash: In a second small bowl, beat together the egg and water. Brush the egg wash on top of each bagel.
6. Generously sprinkle the everything seasoning over the top of the 2 plain bagels.
7. To cook the bagels: Install a crisper plate in each of the two baskets. Place the cinnamon-raisin bagels in the Zone 1 basket and insert the basket in the unit. For best results, the bagels should not overlap in the basket. Place the everything bagels in the Zone 2 basket and insert the basket in the unit.
8. Select Zone 1, select AIR FRY, set the temperature to 325°F, and set the time to 14 minutes. Select MATCH COOK to match Zone 2 settings to Zone 1.
9. Press START/PAUSE to begin cooking.
10. When cooking is complete, use silicone-tipped tongs to transfer the bagels to a cutting board. Let cool for 2 to 3 minutes before cutting and serving.

Nutrition:
- (Per serving) Calories: 238; Total fat: 3g; Saturated fat: 1g; Carbohydrates: 43g; Fiber: 1.5g; Protein: 11g; Sodium: 321mg

Perfect Cinnamon Toast

Servings: 6
Cooking Time: 10 Minutes
Ingredients:
- 12 slices whole-wheat bread
- 1 stick butter, room temperature
- ½ cup white sugar
- 1½ teaspoons ground cinnamon
- 1½ teaspoons pure vanilla extract
- 1 pinch kosher salt
- 2 pinches freshly ground black pepper (optional)

Directions:
1. Mash the softened butter with a fork or the back of a spoon in a bowl. Add the sugar, cinnamon, vanilla, and salt. Stir until everything is well combined.
2. Spread one-sixth of the mixture onto each slice of bread, making sure to cover the entire surface.
3. Install a crisper plate in both drawers. Place half the bread sliced in the zone 1 drawer and half in the zone 2 drawer, then insert the drawers into the unit.
4. Select zone 1, select AIR FRY, set temperature to 400 degrees F/ 200 degrees C, and set time to 5 minutes. Select MATCH to match zone 2 settings to zone 1. Press theSTART/STOP button to begin cooking
5. When cooking is complete, remove the slices and cut them diagonally.
6. Serve immediately.

Nutrition:
- (Per serving) Calories 322 | Fat 16.5g | Sodium 249mg | Carbs 39.3g | Fiber 4.2g | Sugar 18.2g | Protein 8.2g

Yellow Potatoes With Eggs

Servings: 2
Cooking Time: 35
Ingredients:
- 1 pound of Dutch yellow potatoes, quartered
- 1 red bell pepper, chopped
- Salt and black pepper, to taste
- 1 green bell pepper, chopped
- 2 teaspoons of olive oil
- 2 teaspoons of garlic powder
- 1 teaspoon of onion powder
- 1 egg
- ¼ teaspoon of butter

Directions:
1. Toss together diced potatoes, green pepper, red pepper, salt, black pepper, and olive oil along with garlic powder and onion powder.
2. Put in the zone 1 basket of the air fryer.
3. Take ramekin and grease it with oil spray.
4. Whisk egg in a bowl and add salt and pepper along with ½ teaspoon of butter.
5. Pour egg into a ramekin and place it in a zone 2 basket.
6. Now start cooking and set a timer for zone 1 basket to 30-35 minutes at 400 degrees at AIR FRY mode.
7. Now for zone 2, set it on AIR FRY mode at 350 degrees F for 8-10 minutes.
8. Press the Smart finish button and press start, it will finish both at the same time.
9. Once done, serve and enjoy.

Nutrition:
- (Per serving) Calories252 | Fat7.5g | Sodium 37mg | Carbs 40g | Fiber3.9g | Sugar 7g | Protein 6.7g

Mozzarella Bacon Calzones

Servings: 4
Cooking Time: 12 Minutes
Ingredients:
- 2 large eggs
- 235 ml blanched finely ground almond flour
- 475 ml shredded Mozzarella cheese
- 60 g cream cheese, softened and broken into small pieces
- 4 slices cooked bacon, crumbled

Directions:
1. Beat eggs in a small bowl. Pour into a medium nonstick skillet over medium heat and scramble. Set aside.
2. In a large microwave-safe bowl, mix flour and Mozzarella. Add cream cheese to the bowl.
3. Place bowl in microwave and cook 45 seconds on high to melt cheese, then stir with a fork until a soft dough ball forms.
4. Cut a piece of parchment to fit air fryer drawer. Separate dough into two sections and press each out into an 8-inch round.
5. On half of each dough round, place half of the scrambled eggs and crumbled bacon. Fold the other side of the dough over and press to seal the edges.
6. Place calzones on ungreased parchment and into the zone 1 air fryer drawer. Adjust the temperature to 176ºC and set the timer for 12 minutes, turning calzones halfway through cooking. Crust will be golden and firm when done.
7. Let calzones cool on a cooking rack 5 minutes before serving.

Blueberry Coffee Cake And Maple Sausage Patties

Servings: 6
Cooking Time: 25 Minutes

Ingredients:
- FOR THE COFFEE CAKE
- 6 tablespoons unsalted butter, at room temperature, divided
- ⅓ cup granulated sugar
- 1 large egg
- 1 teaspoon vanilla extract
- ¼ cup whole milk
- 1½ cups all-purpose flour, divided
- 1 teaspoon baking powder
- ¼ teaspoon salt
- 1 cup blueberries
- ¼ cup packed light brown sugar
- ½ teaspoon ground cinnamon
- FOR THE SAUSAGE PATTIES
- ½ pound ground pork
- 2 tablespoons maple syrup
- ½ teaspoon dried sage
- ½ teaspoon dried thyme
- 1½ teaspoons kosher salt
- ½ teaspoon crushed fennel seeds
- ½ teaspoon red pepper flakes (optional)
- ¼ teaspoon freshly ground black pepper

Directions:
1. To prep the coffee cake: In a large bowl, cream together 4 tablespoons of butter with the granulated sugar. Beat in the egg, vanilla, and milk.
2. Stir in 1 cup of flour, along with the baking soda and salt, to form a thick batter. Fold in the blueberries.
3. In a second bowl, mix the remaining 2 tablespoons of butter, remaining ½ cup of flour, the brown sugar, and cinnamon to form a dry crumbly mixture.
4. To prep the sausage patties: In a large bowl, mix the pork, maple syrup, sage, thyme, salt, fennel seeds, red pepper flakes (if using), and black pepper until just combined.
5. Divide the mixture into 6 equal patties about ½ inch thick.
6. To cook the coffee cake and sausage patties: Spread the cake batter into the Zone 1 basket, top with the crumble mixture, and insert the basket in the unit. Install a crisper plate in the Zone 2 basket, add the sausage patties in a single layer, and insert the basket in the unit.
7. Select Zone 1, select BAKE, set the temperature to 350°F, and set the time to 25 minutes.
8. Select Zone 2, select AIR FRY, set the temperature to 375°F, and set the time to 12 minutes. Select SMART FINISH.
9. Press START/PAUSE to begin cooking.
10. When the Zone 2 timer reads 6 minutes, press START/PAUSE. Remove the basket and use silicone-tipped tongs to flip the sausage patties. Reinsert the basket and press START/PAUSE to resume cooking.
11. When cooking is complete, let the coffee cake cool for at least 5 minutes, then cut into 6 slices. Serve warm or at room temperature with the sausage patties.

Nutrition:
- (Per serving) Calories: 395; Total fat: 15g; Saturated fat: 8g; Carbohydrates: 53g; Fiber: 1.5g; Protein: 14g; Sodium: 187mg

Quick And Easy Blueberry Muffins

Servings: 8 Muffins
Cooking Time: 12 Minutes

Ingredients:
- 315 ml flour
- 120 ml sugar
- 2 teaspoons baking powder
- ¼ teaspoon salt
- 80 ml rapeseed oil
- 1 egg
- 120 ml milk
- 160 ml blueberries, fresh or frozen and thawed

Directions:
1. Preheat the air fryer to 165°C.
2. In a medium bowl, stir together flour, sugar, baking powder, and salt.
3. In a separate bowl, combine oil, egg, and milk and mix well.
4. Add egg mixture to dry ingredients and stir just until moistened.
5. Gently stir in the blueberries.
6. Spoon batter evenly into parchment paper-lined muffin cups.
7. Put the muffin cups in the two air fryer baskets and bake for 12 minutes or until tops spring back when touched lightly.
8. Serve immediately.

Cheesy Baked Eggs

Servings: 4
Cooking Time: 16 Minutes
Ingredients:
- 4 large eggs
- 57g smoked gouda, shredded
- Everything bagel seasoning, to taste
- Salt and pepper to taste

Directions:
1. Crack one egg in each ramekin.
2. Top the egg with bagel seasoning, black pepper, salt and gouda.
3. Place 2 ramekins in each air fryer basket.
4. Return the air fryer basket 1 to Zone 1, and basket 2 to Zone 2 of the Tefal 2-Basket Air Fryer.
5. Choose the "Air Fry" mode for Zone 1 and set the temperature to 400 degrees F and 16 minutes of cooking time.
6. Select the "MATCH COOK" option to copy the settings for Zone 2.
7. Initiate cooking by pressing the START/PAUSE BUTTON.
8. Serve warm.

Nutrition:
- (Per serving) Calories 190 | Fat 18g |Sodium 150mg | Carbs 0.6g | Fiber 0.4g | Sugar 0.4g | Protein 7.2g

Wholemeal Blueberry Muffins

Servings: 6
Cooking Time: 15 Minutes
Ingredients:
- Olive oil cooking spray
- 120 ml unsweetened applesauce
- 60 ml honey
- 120 ml non-fat plain Greek yoghurt
- 1 teaspoon vanilla extract
- 1 large egg
- 350 ml plus 1 tablespoon wholemeal, divided
- ½ teaspoon baking soda
- ½ teaspoon baking powder
- ½ teaspoon salt
- 120 ml blueberries, fresh or frozen

Directions:
1. Lightly coat the inside of six silicone muffin cups or a six-cup muffin tin with olive oil cooking spray.
2. In a large bowl, combine the applesauce, honey, yoghurt, vanilla, and egg and mix until smooth. Sift in 350 ml of the flour, the baking soda, baking powder, and salt into the wet mixture, then stir until just combined. In a small bowl, toss the blueberries with the remaining 1 tablespoon flour, then fold the mixture into the muffin batter.
3. Divide the mixture evenly among the prepared muffin cups and place into the zone 1 drawer of the air fryer. Bake at 182°C for 12 to 15 minutes, or until golden brown on top and a toothpick inserted into the middle of one of the muffins comes out clean. Allow to cool for 5 minutes before serving.

Lemon-blueberry Muffins

Servings: 6 Muffins
Cooking Time: 20 To 25 Minutes
Ingredients:
- 300 ml almond flour
- 3 tablespoons granulated sweetener
- 1 teaspoon baking powder
- 2 large eggs
- 3 tablespoons melted butter
- 1 tablespoon almond milk
- 1 tablespoon fresh lemon juice
- 120 ml fresh blueberries

Directions:
1. Preheat the zone 1 air fryer drawer to 176°C. Lightly coat 6 silicone muffin cups with vegetable oil. Set aside.
2. In a large mixing bowl, combine the almond flour, sweetener, and baking soda. Set aside.
3. In a separate small bowl, whisk together the eggs, butter, milk, and lemon juice. Add the egg mixture to the flour mixture and stir until just combined. Fold in the blueberries and let the batter sit for 5 minutes.
4. Spoon the muffin batter into the muffin cups, about two-thirds full. Air fry in the zone 1 drawer for 20 to 25 minutes, or until a toothpick inserted into the center of a muffin comes out clean.
5. Remove the drawer from the air fryer and let the muffins cool for about 5 minutes before transferring them to a wire rack to cool completely.

Mexican Breakfast Pepper Rings

Servings: 4
Cooking Time: 10 Minutes
Ingredients:
- Olive oil
- 1 large red, yellow, or orange pepper, cut into four ¾-inch rings
- 4 eggs
- Salt and freshly ground black pepper, to taste
- 2 teaspoons salsa

Directions:
1. Preheat the air fryer to 176°C. Lightly spray two baking pans with olive oil.
2. Place 4 bell pepper rings on the two pans. Crack one egg into each bell pepper ring. Season with salt and black pepper.
3. Spoon ½ teaspoon of salsa on top of each egg.
4. Place the two pans in the two air fryer drawers. Air fry until the yolk is slightly runny, 5 to 6 minutes or until the yolk is fully cooked, 8 to 10 minutes.
5. Serve hot.

Sweet Potato Hash

Servings: 4
Cooking Time: 15 Minutes
Ingredients:
- 3 sweet potatoes, peel & cut into ½-inch pieces
- ½ tsp cinnamon
- 2 tbsp olive oil
- 1 bell pepper, cut into ½-inch pieces
- ½ tsp dried thyme
- ½ tsp nutmeg
- 1 medium onion, cut into ½-inch pieces
- Pepper
- Salt

Directions:
1. In a bowl, toss sweet potatoes with the remaining ingredients.
2. Insert a crisper plate in Tefal air fryer baskets.
3. Add potato mixture in both baskets.
4. Select zone 1 then select "air fry" mode and set the temperature to 355 degrees F for 15 minutes. Press "match" to match zone 2 settings to zone 1. Press "start/stop" to begin.

Nutrition:
- (Per serving) Calories 167 | Fat 7.3g |Sodium 94mg | Carbs 24.9g | Fiber 4.2g | Sugar 6.8g | Protein 2.2g

Roasted Oranges

Servings: 4
Cooking Time: 6 Minutes
Ingredients:
- 2 oranges, halved
- 2 teaspoons honey
- 1 teaspoon cinnamon

Directions:
1. Place the oranges in each air fryer basket.
2. Drizzle honey and cinnamon over the orange halves.
3. Return the air fryer basket 1 to Zone 1, and basket 2 to Zone 2 of the Tefal 2-Basket Air Fryer.
4. Choose the "Air Fry" mode for Zone 1 at 395 degrees F temperature and 6 minutes of cooking time.
5. Select the "MATCH COOK" option to copy the settings for Zone 2.
6. Initiate cooking by pressing the START/PAUSE BUTTON.
7. Serve.

Nutrition:
- (Per serving) Calories 183 | Fat 15g |Sodium 402mg | Carbs 2.5g | Fiber 0.4g | Sugar 1.1g | Protein 10g

Sausage And Cheese Balls

Servings: 16 Balls
Cooking Time: 12 Minutes
Ingredients:
- 450 g pork sausage meat, removed from casings
- 120 ml shredded Cheddar cheese
- 30 g full-fat cream cheese, softened
- 1 large egg

Directions:
1. Mix all ingredients in a large bowl. Form into sixteen balls. Place the balls into the two air fryer drawers.
2. Adjust the temperature to 204°C and air fry for 12 minutes.
3. Shake the drawers two or three times during cooking. Sausage balls will be browned on the outside and have an internal temperature of at least 64°C when completely cooked.
4. Serve warm.

Baked Egg And Mushroom Cups

Servings: 6
Cooking Time: 15 Minutes

Ingredients:
- Olive oil cooking spray
- 6 large eggs
- 1 garlic clove, minced
- ½ teaspoon salt
- ½ teaspoon black pepper
- Pinch red pepper flakes
- 230 g baby mushrooms, sliced
- 235 ml fresh baby spinach
- 2 spring onions, white parts and green parts, diced

Directions:
1. Lightly coat the inside of six silicone muffin cups or a six-cup muffin tin with olive oil cooking spray. In a large bowl, beat the eggs, garlic, salt, pepper, and red pepper flakes for 1 to 2 minutes, or until well combined.
2. Fold in the mushrooms, spinach, and spring onions. Divide the mixture evenly among the muffin cups. Place into the zone 1 drawer.
3. Select Bake button and adjust temperature to 160°C, set time to 12 to 15 minutes and press Start. Remove after the end and allow to cool for 5 minutes before serving.

French Toast Sticks

Servings: 5
Cooking Time: 12 Minutes
Ingredients:
- 10 teaspoons sugar, divided
- 3¼ teaspoons cinnamon, divided
- 3 slices toast
- 1 egg
- 1 egg yolks
- 80ml milk
- 1 teaspoon sugar
- 1 teaspoon brown sugar
- 1 teaspoon vanilla
- ¼ teaspoon cinnamon

Directions:
1. Line either basket "Zone 1" and "Zone 2" with a greased piece of foil.
2. Press your chosen zone - "Zone 1" and "Zone 2" and then rotate the knob to select "Air Fryer".
3. Set the temperature to 175 degrees C, and then set the time for 3 minutes to preheat.
4. Three teaspoons of sugar and 3 teaspoons of cinnamon are whisked together in a shallow bowl. Set aside.
5. Cut each slice of bread in thirds.
6. Combine the eggs, egg yolks, milk, brown sugar, remaining sugar, vanilla, and remaining cinnamon in a shallow pan.
7. Blend everything until it's smooth.
8. Allow the bread to soak in the egg mixture for a few seconds. Flip over and dip the other side.
9. Coat both sides of the bread in the cinnamon-sugar mixture. Place in the basket.
10. Slide the basket into the Air Fryer and set the time for 8 minutes.
11. After cooking time is completed, transfer the bread to a serving plate and serve.

Homemade Toaster Pastries

Servings: 6 Pastries
Cooking Time: 11 Minutes
Ingredients:
- Oil, for spraying
- 1 (425 g) package refrigerated piecrust
- 6 tablespoons jam or preserves of choice
- 475 ml icing sugar
- 3 tablespoons milk
- 1 to 2 tablespoons sprinkles of choice

Directions:
1. Preheat the air fryer to 176°C. Line the zone 1 air fryer drawer with parchment and spray lightly with oil.
2. Cut the piecrust into 12 rectangles, about 3 by 4 inches each. You will need to reroll the dough scraps to get 12 rectangles.
3. Spread 1 tablespoon of jam in the center of 6 rectangles, leaving ¼ inch around the edges.
4. Pour some water into a small bowl. Use your finger to moisten the edge of each rectangle.
5. Top each rectangle with another and use your fingers to press around the edges. Using the tines of a fork, seal the edges of the dough and poke a few holes in the top of each one. Place the pastries in the prepared drawer.
6. Air fry for 11 minutes. Let cool completely.
7. In a medium bowl, whisk together the icing sugar and milk. Spread the icing over the tops of the pastries and add sprinkles. Serve immediately.

Cheesy Scrambled Eggs And Egg And Bacon Muffins

Servings: 3
Cooking Time: 15 Minutes
Ingredients:
- Cheesy Scrambled Eggs:
- 1 teaspoon unsalted butter
- 2 large eggs
- 2 tablespoons milk
- 2 tablespoons shredded Cheddar cheese
- Salt and freshly ground black pepper, to taste
- Egg and Bacon Muffins:
- 2 eggs
- Salt and ground black pepper, to taste
- 1 tablespoon green pesto
- 85 g shredded Cheddar cheese
- 140 g cooked bacon
- 1 spring onion, chopped

Directions:
1. Make the Cheesy Scrambled Eggs :
2. Preheat the zone 1 air fryer basket to 150ºC. Place the butter in a baking pan and cook for 1 to 2 minutes, until melted.
3. In a small bowl, whisk together the eggs, milk, and cheese. Season with salt and black pepper. Transfer the mixture to the pan.
4. Cook in the zone 1 basket for 3 minutes. Stir the eggs and push them toward the center of the pan.
5. Cook for another 2 minutes, then stir again. Cook for another 2 minutes, until the eggs are just cooked. Serve warm.
6. Make the Egg and Bacon Muffins :
7. Preheat the zone 2 air fryer basket to 175ºC. Line a cupcake tin with parchment paper.
8. Beat the eggs with pepper, salt, and pesto in a bowl. Mix in the cheese.
9. Pour the eggs into the cupcake tin and top with the bacon and spring onion.
10. Bake in the preheated zone 2 air fryer basket for 15 minutes, or until the egg is set.
11. Serve immediately.

anadian Bacon Muffin Sandwiches And All-in-one Toast

Servings: 5
Cooking Time: 10 Minutes
Ingredients:
- Canadian Bacon Muffin Sandwiches:
- 4 English muffins, split
- 8 slices back bacon
- 4 slices cheese
- Cooking spray
- All-in-One Toast:
- 1 strip bacon, diced
- 1 slice 1-inch thick bread
- 1 egg
- Salt and freshly ground black pepper, to taste
- 60 ml grated Monterey Jack or Chedday cheese

Directions:
1. Make the Canadian Bacon Muffin Sandwiches :
2. 1. Preheat the air fryer to 190ºC. Make the sandwiches: Top each of 4 muffin halves with 2 slices of bacon, 1 slice of cheese, and finish with the remaining muffin half. 3. Put the sandwiches in the zone 1 air fryer basket and spritz the tops with cooking spray. 4. Bake for 4 minutes. Flip the sandwiches and bake for another 4 minutes. 5. Divide the sandwiches among four plates and serve warm.
3. Make the All-in-One Toast :
4. Preheat the air fryer to 205ºC.
5. Air fry the bacon in zone 2 basket for 3 minutes, shaking the basket once or twice while it cooks. Remove the bacon to a paper towel lined plate and set aside.
6. Use a sharp paring knife to score a large circle in the middle of the slice of bread, cutting halfway through, but not all the way through to the cutting board. Press down on the circle in the center of the bread slice to create an indentation.
7. Transfer the slice of bread, hole side up, to the zone 2 air fryer basket. Crack the egg into the center of the bread, and season with salt and pepper.
8. Adjust the air fryer temperature to 190ºC and air fry for 5 minutes. Sprinkle the grated cheese around the edges of the bread, leaving the center of the yolk uncovered, and top with the cooked bacon. Press the cheese and bacon into the bread lightly to help anchor it to the bread and prevent it from blowing around in the air fryer.
9. Air fry for one or two more minutes, just to melt the cheese and finish cooking the egg. Serve immediately.

Pumpkin French Toast Casserole With Sweet And Spicy Twisted Bacon

Servings:4
Cooking Time: 35 Minutes
Ingredients:
- FOR THE FRENCH TOAST CASSEROLE
- 3 large eggs
- 1 cup unsweetened almond milk
- 1 cup canned unsweetened pumpkin puree
- 2 teaspoons pumpkin pie spice
- ¼ cup packed light brown sugar
- 1 teaspoon vanilla extract
- 6 cups French bread cubes
- 1 teaspoon vegetable oil
- ¼ cup maple syrup
- FOR THE BACON
- 2 tablespoons light brown sugar
- ⅛ teaspoon cayenne pepper
- 8 slices bacon

Directions:
1. To prep the French toast casserole: In a shallow bowl, whisk together the eggs, almond milk, pumpkin puree, pumpkin pie spice, brown sugar, and vanilla.
2. Add the bread cubes to the egg mixture, making sure the bread is fully coated in the custard. Let sit for at least 10 minutes to allow the bread to soak up the custard.
3. To prep the bacon: In a small bowl, combine the brown sugar and cayenne.
4. Arrange the bacon on a cutting board in a single layer. Evenly sprinkle the strips with the brown sugar mixture. Fold the bacon strip in half lengthwise. Hold one end of the bacon steady and twist the other end so the bacon resembles a straw.
5. To cook the casserole and bacon: Brush the Zone 1 basket with the oil. Pour the French toast casserole into the Zone 1 basket, drizzle with maple syrup, and insert the basket in the unit. Install a crisper plate in the Zone 2 basket, add the bacon twists in a single layer, and insert the basket in the unit. For the best fit, arrange the bacon twists across the unit, front to back.
6. Select Zone 1, select BAKE, set the temperature to 330°F, and set the time to 35 minutes.
7. Select Zone 2, select AIR FRY, set the temperature to 400°F, and set the time to 12 minutes. Select SMART FINISH.
8. Press START/PAUSE to begin cooking.
9. When cooking is complete, transfer the bacon to a plate lined with paper towels. Let cool for 2 to 3 minutes before serving with the French toast casserole.

Nutrition:
- (Per serving) Calories: 601; Total fat: 28g; Saturated fat: 9g; Carbohydrates: 67g; Fiber: 2.5g; Protein: 17g; Sodium: 814mg

Egg And Avocado In The Tefal

Servings:2
Cooking Time:12
Ingredients:
- 2 Avocados, pitted and cut in half
- Garlic salt, to taste
- Cooking for greasing
- 4 eggs
- ¼ teaspoon of Paprika powder, for sprinkling
- 1/3 cup parmesan cheese, crumbled
- 6 bacon strips, raw

Directions:
1. First cut the avocado in half and pit it.
2. Now scoop out the flesh from the avocado and keep intact some of it
3. Crack one egg in each hole of avocado and sprinkle paprika and garlic salt
4. Top it with cheese at the end.
5. Now put it into tin foils and then put it in the air fryer zone basket 1
6. Put bacon strips in zone 2 basket.
7. Now for zone 1, set it to AIR FRY mode at 350 degrees F for 10 minutes
8. And for zone 2, set it 400 degrees for 12 minutes AIR FRY mode.
9. Press the Smart finish button and press start, it will finish both at the same time.
10. Once done, serve and enjoy.

Nutrition:
- (Per serving) Calories609 | Fat53.2g | Sodium 335mg | Carbs 18.1g | Fiber13.5g | Sugar 1.7g | Protein 21.3g

Eggs In Avocado Cups

Servings: 4
Cooking Time: 12 Minutes
Ingredients:
- 2 avocados, halved and pitted
- 4 eggs
- Salt and ground black pepper, as required

Directions:
1. Line either basket of "Zone 1" and "Zone 2" of Tefal 2-Basket Air Fryer with a greased square piece of foil.
2. Press your chosen zone - "Zone 1" and "Zone 2" and then rotate the knob to select "Bake".
3. Set the temperature to 200 degrees C and then set the time for 5 minutes to preheat.
4. Meanwhile, carefully scoop out about 2 teaspoons of flesh from each avocado half.
5. Crack 1 egg in each avocado half and sprinkle with salt and black pepper.
6. After preheating, arrange 2 avocado halves into the basket.
7. Slide the basket into the Air Fryer and set the time for 12 minutes.
8. After cooking time is completed, transfer the avocado halves and onto serving plates and serve hot.
9. **C**

Vanilla Strawberry Doughnuts

Servings: 8
Cooking Time: 15 Minutes
Ingredients:
- 1 egg
- ½ cup strawberries, diced
- 80ml cup milk
- 1 tsp cinnamon
- 1 tsp baking soda
- 136g all-purpose flour
- 2 tsp vanilla
- 2 tbsp butter, melted
- 73g sugar
- ½ tsp salt

Directions:
1. In a bowl, mix flour, cinnamon, baking soda, sugar, and salt.
2. In a separate bowl, whisk egg, milk, butter, and vanilla.
3. Pour egg mixture into the flour mixture and mix until well combined.
4. Add strawberries and mix well.
5. Pour batter into the silicone doughnut moulds.
6. Insert a crisper plate in the Tefal air fryer baskets.
7. Place doughnut moulds in both baskets.
8. Select zone 1, then select "air fry" mode and set the temperature to 320 degrees F for 15 minutes. Press "match" to match zone 2 settings to zone 1. Press "start/stop" to begin.

Nutrition:
- (Per serving) Calories 133 | Fat 3.8g |Sodium 339mg | Carbs 21.9g | Fiber 0.8g | Sugar 9.5g | Protein 2.7g

Turkey Ham Muffins

Servings: 16
Cooking Time: 10 Minutes
Ingredients:
- 1 egg
- 340g all-purpose flour
- 85g turkey ham, chopped
- 2 tbsp mix herbs, chopped
- 235g cheddar cheese, shredded
- 1 onion, chopped
- 2 tsp baking powder
- 2 tbsp butter, melted
- 237ml milk
- Pepper
- Salt

Directions:
1. In a large bowl, mix flour and baking powder.
2. Add egg, butter, and milk and mix until well combined.
3. Add herbs, cheese, onion, and turkey ham and mix well.
4. Insert a crisper plate in the Tefal air fryer baskets.
5. Pour the batter into the silicone muffin moulds.
6. Place muffin moulds in both baskets.
7. Select zone 1, then select "air fry" mode and set the temperature to 355 degrees F for 10 minutes. Press "match" to match zone 2 settings to zone 1. Press "start/stop" to begin.

Nutrition:
- (Per serving) Calories 140 | Fat 4.8g |Sodium 126mg | Carbs 18.2g | Fiber 0.7g | Sugar 1.2g | Protein 5.8g

Air Fried Sausage

Servings: 4
Cooking Time: 13 Minutes.
Ingredients:
- 4 sausage links, raw and uncooked

Directions:
1. Divide the sausages in the two crisper plates.
2. Return the crisper plate to the Tefal Dual Zone Air Fryer.
3. Choose the Air Fry mode for Zone 1 and set the temperature to 390 degrees F and set the time to 13 minutes.
4. Select the "MATCH" button to copy the settings for Zone 2.
5. Initiate cooking by pressing the START/STOP button.
6. Serve warm and fresh.

Nutrition:
- (Per serving) Calories 267 | Fat 12g |Sodium 165mg | Carbs 39g | Fiber 1.4g | Sugar 22g | Protein 3.3g

Sausage And Egg Breakfast Burrito

Servings: 6
Cooking Time: 30 Minutes
Ingredients:
- 6 eggs
- Salt and pepper, to taste
- Cooking oil
- 120 ml chopped red pepper
- 120 ml chopped green pepper
- 230 g chicken sausage meat (removed from casings)
- 120 ml salsa
- 6 medium (8-inch) flour tortillas
- 120 ml shredded Cheddar cheese

Directions:
1. In a medium bowl, whisk the eggs. Add salt and pepper to taste.
2. Place a skillet on medium-high heat. Spray with cooking oil. Add the eggs. Scramble for 2 to 3 minutes, until the eggs are fluffy. Remove the eggs from the skillet and set aside.
3. If needed, spray the skillet with more oil. Add the chopped red and green bell peppers. Cook for 2 to 3 minutes, until the peppers are soft.
4. Add the sausage meat to the skillet. Break the sausage into smaller pieces using a spatula or spoon. Cook for 3 to 4 minutes, until the sausage is brown.
5. Add the salsa and scrambled eggs. Stir to combine. Remove the skillet from heat.
6. Spoon the mixture evenly onto the tortillas.
7. To form the burritos, fold the sides of each tortilla in toward the middle and then roll up from the bottom. You can secure each burrito with a toothpick. Or you can moisten the outside edge of the tortilla with a small amount of water. I prefer to use a cooking brush, but you can also dab with your fingers.
8. Spray the burritos with cooking oil and place them in the two air fryer drawers. Do not stack. Air fry at 204ºC for 8 minutes.
9. Open the air fryer and flip the burritos. Cook for an additional 2 minutes or until crisp.
10. Sprinkle the Cheddar cheese over the burritos. Cool before serving.

Bagels

Servings: 8
Cooking Time: 15 Minutes
Ingredients:
- 2 cups self-rising flour
- 2 cups non-fat plain Greek yogurt
- 2 beaten eggs for egg wash (optional)
- ½ cup sesame seeds (optional)

Directions:
1. In a medium mixing bowl, combine the self-rising flour and Greek yogurt using a wooden spoon.
2. Knead the dough for about 5 minutes on a lightly floured board.
3. Divide the dough into four equal pieces and roll each into a thin rope, securing the ends to form a bagel shape.
4. Install a crisper plate in both drawers. Place 4 bagels in a single layer in each drawer. Insert the drawers into the unit.
5. Select zone 1, select AIR FRY, set temperature to 360 degrees F/ 180 degrees C, and set time to 15 minutes. Select MATCH to match zone 2 settings to zone 1. Select START/STOP to begin.
6. Once the timer has finished, remove the bagels from the units.
7. Serve and enjoy!

Nutrition:
- (Per serving) Calories 202 | Fat 4.5g | Sodium 55mg | Carbs 31.3g | Fiber 2.7g | Sugar 4.7g | Protein 8.7g

Breakfast Calzone And Western Frittata

Servings: 5
Cooking Time: 20 Minutes
Ingredients:
- Breakfast Calzone:
- 350 ml shredded Mozzarella cheese
- 120 ml blanched finely ground almond flour
- 30 g full-fat cream cheese
- 1 large whole egg
- 4 large eggs, scrambled
- 230 g cooked sausage meat, removed from casings and crumbled
- 8 tablespoons shredded mild Cheddar cheese
- Western Frittata:
- ½ red or green pepper, cut into ½-inch chunks
- 1 teaspoon olive oil
- 3 eggs, beaten
- 60 ml grated Cheddar cheese
- 60 ml diced cooked ham
- Salt and freshly ground black pepper, to taste
- 1 teaspoon butter
- 1 teaspoon chopped fresh parsley

Directions:
1. Make the Breakfast Calzone :
2. In a large microwave-safe bowl, add Mozzarella, almond flour, and cream cheese. Microwave for 1 minute. Stir until the mixture is smooth and forms a ball. Add the egg and stir until dough forms.
3. Place dough between two sheets of parchment and roll out to ¼-inch thickness. Cut the dough into four rectangles.
4. Mix scrambled eggs and cooked sausage together in a large bowl. Divide the mixture evenly among each piece of dough, placing it on the lower half of the rectangle. Sprinkle each with 2 tablespoons Cheddar.
5. Fold over the rectangle to cover the egg and meat mixture. Pinch, roll, or use a wet fork to close the edges completely.
6. Cut a piece of parchment to fit your air fryer drawer and place the calzones onto the parchment. Place parchment into the zone 1 air fryer drawer.
7. Adjust the temperature to 192°C and air fry for 15 minutes.
8. Flip the calzones halfway through the cooking time. When done, calzones should be golden in color. Serve immediately.
9. Make the Western Frittata :
10. Preheat the zone 2 air fryer drawer to 204°C.
11. Toss the peppers with the olive oil and air fry for 6 minutes, shaking the drawer once or twice during the cooking process to redistribute the ingredients.
12. While the vegetables are cooking, beat the eggs well in a bowl, stir in the Cheddar cheese and ham, and season with salt and freshly ground black pepper. Add the air-fried peppers to this bowl when they have finished cooking.
13. Place a cake pan into the zone 2 air fryer drawer with the butter, using an aluminum sling to lower the pan into the drawer. Air fry for 1 minute at 192°C to melt the butter. Remove the cake pan and rotate the pan to distribute the butter and grease the pan. Pour the egg mixture into the cake pan and return the pan to the air fryer, using the aluminum sling.
14. Air fry at 192°C for 12 minutes, or until the frittata has puffed up and is lightly browned. Let the frittata sit in the air fryer for 5 minutes to cool to an edible temperature and set up. Remove the cake pan from the air fryer, sprinkle with parsley and serve immediately.

Bacon & Spinach Cups

Servings: 6
Cooking Time: 19 Minutes
Ingredients:
- 6 eggs
- 12 bacon slices, chopped
- 120g fresh baby spinach
- 180g heavy cream
- 6 tablespoons Parmesan cheese, grated
- Salt and ground black pepper, as required

Directions:
1. Heat a non-stick frying pan over medium-high heat and cook the bacon for about 6-8 minutes.
2. Add the spinach and cook for about 2-3 minutes.
3. Stir in the heavy cream and Parmesan cheese and cook for about 2-3 minutes.
4. Remove from the heat and set aside to cool slightly.
5. Press "Zone 1" and "Zone 2" of Tefal 2-Basket Air Fryer and then rotate the knob for each zone to select "Air Fry".
6. Set the temperature to 175 degrees C and then set the time for 5 minutes to preheat.
7. Crack 1 egg in each of 6 greased ramekins and top with bacon mixture.
8. After preheating, arrange 3 ramekins into the basket of each zone.
9. Slide the basket into the Air Fryer and set the time for 5 minutes.
10. After cooking time is completed, remove the ramekins from Air Fryer.
11. Sprinkle the top of each cup with salt and black pepper and serve hot.

Banana Bread

Servings: 8
Cooking Time: 35 Minutes
Ingredients:
- 95g flour
- 1 teaspoon ground cinnamon
- ¼ teaspoon ground nutmeg
- ½ teaspoon salt
- ¼ teaspoon baking soda
- 2 medium-sized ripe bananas mashed
- 2 large eggs lightly beaten
- 100g granulated sugar
- 2 tablespoons whole milk
- 1 tablespoon plain nonfat yoghurt
- 2 tablespoons vegetable oil
- 1 teaspoon vanilla
- 2 tablespoons walnuts roughly chopped

Directions:
1. Combine flour, cinnamon, nutmeg, baking soda, and salt in a large mixing basin.
2. Mash the banana in a separate dish before adding the eggs, sugar, milk, yoghurt, oil, and vanilla extract.
3. Combine the wet and dry ingredients in a mixing bowl and stir until just incorporated.
4. Pour the batter into the loaf pan and top with chopped walnuts.
5. Press either "Zone 1" and "Zone 2" and then rotate the knob select "Air Fryer".
6. Set the temperature to 155 degrees C, and then set the time for 3 minutes to preheat.
7. After preheating, arrange 1 loaf pan into the basket.
8. Slide basket into Air Fryer and set the time for 35 minutes.
9. After cooking time is completed, remove pan from Air Fryer.
10. Place the loaf pan onto a wire rack to cool for about 10 minutes.
11. Carefully invert the bread onto a wire rack to cool completely before slicing
12. Cut the bread into desired-sized slices and serve.

Snacks And Appetizers Recipes

Croquettes

Servings: 6
Cooking Time: 10 Minutes
Ingredients:
- 460g mashed potatoes
- 50g grated Parmesan cheese
- 50g shredded Swiss cheese
- 1 shallot, finely chopped
- 2 teaspoons minced fresh rosemary
- ½ teaspoon salt
- ¼ teaspoon pepper
- 420g finely chopped cooked turkey
- 1 large egg
- 2 tablespoons water
- 110g panko bread crumbs
- Cooking spray

Directions:
1. Combine mashed potatoes, cheeses, shallot, rosemary, salt, and pepper in a large mixing bowl| stir in turkey.
2. Lightly but completely combine the ingredients. Form into twelve 5cm thick patties.
3. Whisk the egg and water together in a small basin. In a shallow bowl, place the bread crumbs.
4. Dip the croquettes in the egg mixture, then in the bread crumbs, patting them down.
5. Press either "Zone 1" or "Zone 2" and then rotate the knob to select "Air Fry".
6. Set the temperature to 190 degrees C, and then set the time for 5 minutes to preheat.
7. After preheating, spray the Air-Fryer basket with cooking spray and line with parchment paper. Arrange in a single layer and spritz them with cooking spray.
8. Slide the basket into the Air Fryer and set the time for 5 minutes.
9. After that, turn them and again cook for 5 minutes longer.
10. After cooking time is completed, transfer them onto serving plates and serve.

Blueberries Muffins

Servings: 2
Cooking Time: 15
Ingredients:
- Salt, pinch
- 2 eggs
- 1/3 cup sugar
- 1/3 cup vegetable oil
- 4 tablespoons of water
- 1 teaspoon of lemon zest
- ¼ teaspoon of vanilla extract
- ½ teaspoon of baking powder
- 1 cup all-purpose flour
- 1 cup blueberries

Directions:
1. Take 4 one-cup sized ramekins that are oven safe and layer them with muffin papers.
2. Take a bowl and whisk the egg, sugar, oil, water, vanilla extract, and lemon zest.
3. Whisk it all very well.
4. Now, in a separate bowl, mix the flour, baking powder, and salt.
5. Now, add dry ingredients slowly to wet ingredients.
6. Now, pour this batter into ramekins and top it with blueberries.
7. Now, divide it between both zones of the Tefale 2-Basket Air Fryer.
8. Set the time for zone 1 to 15 minutes at 350 degrees F.
9. Select the MATCH button for the zone 2 basket.
10. Check if not done, and let it AIR FRY for one more minute.
11. Once it is done, serve.

Nutrition:
- (Per serving) Calories 781| Fat41.6g | Sodium 143mg | Carbs 92.7g | Fiber 3.5g| Sugar41.2 g | Protein 0g

Buffalo Wings Honey-garlic Wings

Servings: 6
Cooking Time: 40 Minutes
Ingredients:
- FOR THE BUFFALO WINGS
- 2 pounds chicken wings
- ¼ teaspoon kosher salt
- ¼ teaspoon freshly ground black pepper
- ¼ teaspoon paprika
- 1 tablespoon vegetable oil
- ⅓ cup Buffalo wing sauce
- FOR THE HONEY-GARLIC WINGS
- 2 pounds chicken wings
- 2 tablespoons all-purpose flour
- ½ teaspoon garlic powder
- 1 tablespoon vegetable oil
- ¼ cup honey
- 2 tablespoons reduced-sodium soy sauce
- ½ teaspoon ground ginger (optional)

Directions:
1. To prep the Buffalo wings: In a large bowl, combine the wings, salt, black pepper, and paprika and toss to coat the wings with the seasonings. Drizzle with the oil.
2. To prep the honey-garlic wings: In another large bowl, combine the wings, flour, and garlic powder and toss to coat the wings. Drizzle with the oil.
3. In a small bowl, whisk together the honey, soy sauce, and ginger (if using). Set the honey-soy sauce aside.
4. To cook the wings: Install a crisper plate in each of the two baskets. Place the Buffalo wings in the Zone 1 basket and insert the basket in the unit. Place the honey-garlic wings in the Zone 2 basket and insert the basket in the unit.
5. Select Zone 1, select AIR FRY, set the temperature to 390°F, and set the time to 40 minutes. Select MATCH COOK to match Zone 2 settings to Zone 1.
6. Press START/PAUSE to begin cooking.
7. When both timers read 8 minutes, press START/PAUSE. Remove the Zone 1 basket, drizzle the Buffalo sauce over the wings, and shake to coat the wings with the sauce. Reinsert the basket. Remove the Zone 2 basket, drizzle the honey-soy sauce over the wings, and shake to coat the wings with the sauce. Reinsert the basket. Press START/PAUSE to resume cooking.
8. When cooking is complete, the wings will be golden brown and cooked through. Use silicone-tipped tongs to transfer the wings to a serving plate. Serve warm.

Nutrition:
- (Per serving) Calories: 399; Total fat: 28g; Saturated fat: 7.5g; Carbohydrates: 0g; Fiber: 0g; Protein: 34g; Sodium: 1,049mg

Tangy Fried Pickle Spears

Servings: 6
Cooking Time: 15 Minutes
Ingredients:
- 2 jars sweet and sour pickle spears, patted dry
- 2 medium-sized eggs
- 80 ml milk
- 1 teaspoon garlic powder
- 1 teaspoon sea salt
- ½ teaspoon shallot powder
- ⅓ teaspoon chilli powder
- 80 ml plain flour
- Cooking spray

Directions:
1. Preheat the air fryer to 195°C. Spritz the zone 1 air fryer basket with cooking spray.
2. In a bowl, beat together the eggs with milk. In another bowl, combine garlic powder, sea salt, shallot powder, chilli powder and plain flour until well blended.
3. One by one, roll the pickle spears in the powder mixture, then dredge them in the egg mixture. Dip them in the powder mixture a second time for additional coating.
4. Arrange the coated pickles in the prepared basket. Air fry for 15 minutes until golden and crispy, shaking the basket halfway through to ensure even cooking.
5. Transfer to a plate and let cool for 5 minutes before serving.

Goat Cheese And Garlic Crostini & Sweet Bacon Potato Crunchies

Servings: 8
Cooking Time: 7 Minutes
Ingredients:
- Goat Cheese and Garlic Crostini:
- 1 wholemeal baguette
- 60 ml olive oil
- 2 garlic cloves, minced
- 113 g goat cheese
- 2 tablespoons fresh basil, minced
- Sweet Bacon Potato Crunchies:
- 24 frozen potato crunchies
- 6 slices cooked bacon
- 2 tablespoons maple syrup
- 240 ml shredded Cheddar cheese

Directions:
1. Make the Goat Cheese and Garlic Crostini :
2. Preheat the air fryer to 190°C.
3. Cut the baguette into ½-inch-thick slices.
4. In a small bowl, mix together the olive oil and garlic, then brush it over one side of each slice of bread.
5. Place the olive-oil-coated bread in a single layer in the zone 1 air fryer basket and bake for 5 minutes.
6. Meanwhile, in a small bowl, mix together the goat cheese and basil.
7. Remove the toast from the air fryer, then spread a thin layer of the goat cheese mixture over the top of each piece and serve.
8. Make the Sweet Bacon Potato Crunchies :
9. Preheat the air fryer to 205°C.
10. Put the potato crunchies in the zone 2 air fryer basket. Air fry for 10 minutes, shaking the basket halfway through the cooking time.
11. Meanwhile, cut the bacon into 1-inch pieces.
12. Remove the potato crunchies from the air fryer basket and put into a baking pan. Top with the bacon and drizzle with the maple syrup. Air fry for 5 minutes, or until the crunchies and bacon are crisp.
13. Top with the cheese and air fry for 2 minutes, or until the cheese is melted.
14. Serve hot.

Waffle Fries

Servings: 2
Cooking Time: 15 Minutes
Ingredients:
- 2 russet potatoes
- ½ teaspoon seasoning salt

Directions:
1. If desired, peel the potatoes.
2. With Wave-Waffle Cutter, slice potatoes by turning them one-quarter turn after each pass over the blade.
3. In a mixing dish, toss the potato pieces with the seasoning salt. Toss the potatoes in the seasoning to ensure that it is uniformly distributed.
4. Place a baking sheet on the baskets.
5. Press either "Zone 1" or "Zone 2" and then rotate the knob to select "Air Fryer".
6. Set the temperature to 200 degrees C, and then set the time for 5 minutes to preheat.
7. After preheating, arrange them into the basket.
8. Slide the basket into the Air Fryer and set the time for 15 minutes.
9. After cooking time is completed, place on a wire rack for a few minutes, then transfer onto serving plates and serve.

Cheese Stuffed Mushrooms

Servings: 4
Cooking Time: 10 Minutes
Ingredients:
- 176g button mushrooms, clean & cut stems
- 46g sour cream
- 17g cream cheese, softened
- ½ tsp garlic powder
- 58g cheddar cheese, shredded
- Pepper
- Salt

Directions:
1. In a small bowl, mix cream cheese, garlic powder, sour cream, pepper, and salt.
2. Stuff cream cheese mixture into each mushroom and top each with cheddar cheese.
3. Insert a crisper plate in the Tefal air fryer baskets.
4. Place the stuffed mushrooms in both baskets.
5. Select zone 1 then select "air fry" mode and set the temperature to 370 degrees F for 8 minutes. Press "match" to match zone 2 settings to zone 1. Press "start/stop" to begin.

Chicken Tenders

Servings:3
Cooking Time:12
Ingredients:
- 1 pound of chicken tender
- Salt and black pepper, to taste
- 1 cup Panko bread crumbs
- 2 cups Italian bread crumbs
- 1 cup parmesan cheese
- 2 eggs
- Oil spray, for greasing

Directions:
1. Sprinkle the tenders with salt and black pepper.
2. In a medium bowl mix Panko bread crumbs with Italian breadcrumbs.
3. Add salt, pepper, and parmesan cheese.
4. Crack two eggs in a bowl.
5. First, put the chicken tender in eggs.
6. Now dredge the tender in a bowl and coat the tender well with crumbs.
7. Line both of the baskets of the air fryer with parchment paper.
8. At the end spray the tenders with oil spray.
9. Divided the tenders between the baskets of Tefale 2-Basket Air Fryer.
10. Set zone 1 basket to AIR FRY mode at 350 degrees F for 12 minutes.
11. Select the MATCH button for the zone 2 basket.
12. Once it's done, serve.

Nutrition:
- (Per serving) Calories558 | Fat23.8g | Sodium872 mg | Carbs 20.9g | Fiber1.7 g| Sugar2.2 g | Protein 63.5g

Crispy Plantain Chips

Servings: 4
Cooking Time: 20 Minutes.
Ingredients:
- 1 green plantain
- 1 teaspoon canola oil
- ½ teaspoon sea salt

Directions:
1. Peel and cut the plantains into long strips using a mandolin slicer.
2. Grease the crisper plates with ½ teaspoon of canola oil.
3. Toss the plantains with salt and remaining canola oil.
4. Divide these plantains in the two crisper plates.
5. Return the crisper plate to the Tefal Dual Zone Air Fryer.
6. Choose the Air Fry mode for Zone 1 and set the temperature to 350 degrees F and the time to 20 minutes.
7. Select the "MATCH" button to copy the settings for Zone 2.
8. Initiate cooking by pressing the START/STOP button.
9. Toss the plantains after 10 minutes and resume cooking.
10. Serve warm.

Nutrition:
- (Per serving) Calories 122 | Fat 1.8g |Sodium 794mg | Carbs 17g | Fiber 8.9g | Sugar 1.6g | Protein 14.9g

Cauliflower Gnocchi

Servings: 5
Cooking Time: 17 Minutes.
Ingredients:
- 1 bag frozen cauliflower gnocchi
- 1 ½ tablespoons olive oil
- 1 teaspoon garlic powder
- 3 tablespoons parmesan, grated
- ½ teaspoon dried basil
- Salt to taste
- Fresh chopped parsley for topping

Directions:
1. Toss gnocchi with olive oil, garlic powder, 1 tablespoon of parmesan, salt, and basil in a bowl.
2. Divide the gnocchi in the two crisper plate.
3. Return the crisper plate to the Tefal Dual Zone Air Fryer.
4. Choose the Air Fry mode for Zone 1 and set the temperature to 400 degrees F and the time to 10 minutes.
5. Select the "MATCH" button to copy the settings for Zone 2.
6. Initiate cooking by pressing the START/STOP button.
7. Toss the gnocchi once cooked halfway through, then resume cooking.
8. Drizzle the remaining parmesan on top of the gnocchi and cook again for 7 minutes.
9. Serve warm.

Nutrition:
- (Per serving) Calories 134 | Fat 5.9g |Sodium 343mg | Carbs 9.5g | Fiber 0.5g | Sugar 1.1g | Protein 10.4g

Healthy Spinach Balls

Servings: 4
Cooking Time: 15 Minutes
Ingredients:
- 1 egg
- 29g breadcrumbs
- ½ medium onion, chopped
- 225g spinach, blanched & chopped
- 1 carrot, peel & grated
- 1 tbsp cornflour
- 1 tbsp nutritional yeast
- 1 tsp garlic, minced
- ½ tsp garlic powder
- Pepper
- Salt

Directions:
1. Add spinach and remaining ingredients into the mixing bowl and mix until well combined.
2. Insert a crisper plate in the Tefal air fryer baskets.
3. Make small balls from the spinach mixture and place them in both baskets.
4. Select zone 1, then select "air fry" mode and set the temperature to 390 degrees F for 10 minutes. Press "match" to match zone 2 settings to zone 1. Press "start/stop" to begin.

Beef Skewers

Servings: 6
Cooking Time: 5 Minutes
Ingredients:
- 1 beef flank steak
- 240ml rice vinegar
- 240ml soy sauce
- 55g packed brown sugar
- 2 tablespoons minced fresh gingerroot
- 6 garlic cloves, minced
- 3 teaspoons sesame oil
- 1 teaspoon hot pepper sauce
- ½ teaspoon cornflour

Directions:
1. Cut beef into ½ cm thick strips. Whisk together the following 7 ingredients in a large mixing bowl until well combined.
2. In a shallow dish, pour 1 cup of marinade. Toss in the beef and turn to coat. Refrigerate for 2-8 hours, covered. Cover and keep the remaining marinade refrigerated.
3. Beef should be drained. 12 metal or wet wooden skewers threaded with beef.
4. Press either "Zone 1" or "Zone 2" and then rotate the knob to select "Air Fry".
5. Set the temperature to 200 degrees C, and then set the time for 5 minutes to preheat.
6. After preheating, spray the basket with cooking spray and arrange skewers onto basket.
7. Slide the basket into the Air Fryer and set the time for 5 minutes.
8. After cooking time is completed, transfer them onto serving plates and serve.

Pepperoni Pizza Dip

Servings: 6
Cooking Time: 10 Minutes
Ingredients:
- 170 g soft white cheese
- 177 ml shredded Italian cheese blend
- 60 ml sour cream
- 1½ teaspoons dried Italian seasoning
- ¼ teaspoon garlic salt
- ¼ teaspoon onion powder
- 177 ml pizza sauce
- 120 ml sliced miniature pepperoni
- 60 ml sliced black olives
- 1 tablespoon thinly sliced green onion
- Cut-up raw vegetables, toasted baguette slices, pitta chips, or tortilla chips, for serving

Directions:
1. In a small bowl, combine the soft white cheese, 60 ml of the shredded cheese, the sour cream, Italian seasoning, garlic salt, and onion powder. Stir until smooth and the ingredients are well blended.
2. Spread the mixture in a baking pan. Top with the pizza sauce, spreading to the edges. Sprinkle with the remaining 120 ml shredded cheese. Arrange the pepperoni slices on top of the cheese. Top with the black olives and green onion.
3. Place the pan in the zone 1 air fryer basket. Set the air fryer to 175°C for 10 minutes, or until the pepperoni is beginning to brown on the edges and the cheese is bubbly and lightly browned.
4. Let stand for 5 minutes before serving with vegetables, toasted baguette slices, pitta chips, or tortilla chips.

Ravioli

Servings: 2
Cooking Time: 6 Minutes
Ingredients:
- 12 frozen portions of ravioli
- ½ cup buttermilk
- ½ cup Italian breadcrumbs

Directions:
1. Place two bowls side by side. Put the buttermilk in one and breadcrumbs in the other.
2. Dip each piece of ravioli into the buttermilk then breadcrumbs, making sure to coat them as best as possible.
3. Place a crisper plate in both drawers. In each drawer, put four breaded ravioli pieces in a single layer. Insert the drawers into the unit.
4. Select zone 1, then AIR FRY, then set the temperature to 360 degrees F/ 180 degrees C with a 6-minute timer. To match zone 2 settings to zone 1, choose MATCH. To begin, select START/STOP.
5. Remove the ravioli from the drawers after the timer has finished.

Nutrition:
- (Per serving) Calories 481 | Fat 20g | Sodium 1162mg | Carbs 56g | Fiber 4g | Sugar 9g | Protein 19g

Shrimp Pirogues

Servings: 8
Cooking Time: 4 To 5 Minutes
Ingredients:
- 340 g small, peeled, and deveined raw shrimp
- 85 g soft white cheese, room temperature
- 2 tablespoons natural yoghurt
- 1 teaspoon lemon juice
- 1 teaspoon dried dill weed, crushed
- Salt, to taste
- 4 small hothouse cucumbers, each approximately 6 inches long

Directions:
1. Pour 4 tablespoons water in bottom of air fryer drawer.
2. Place shrimp in air fryer basket in single layer and air fry at 200°C for 4 to 5 minutes, just until done. Watch carefully because shrimp cooks quickly, and overcooking makes it tough.
3. Chop shrimp into small pieces, no larger than ½ inch. Refrigerate while mixing the remaining ingredients.
4. With a fork, mash and whip the soft white cheese until smooth.
5. Stir in the yoghurt and beat until smooth. Stir in lemon juice, dill weed, and chopped shrimp.
6. Taste for seasoning. If needed, add ¼ to ½ teaspoon salt to suit your taste.
7. Store in refrigerator until serving time.
8. When ready to serve, wash and dry cucumbers and split them lengthwise. Scoop out the seeds and turn cucumbers upside down on paper towels to drain for 10 minutes.
9. Just before filling, wipe centres of cucumbers dry. Spoon the shrimp mixture into the pirogues and cut in half crosswise. Serve immediately.

Healthy Chickpea Fritters

Servings: 6
Cooking Time: 5 Minutes
Ingredients:
- 1 egg
- 425g can chickpeas, rinsed & drained
- ½ tsp ground ginger
- ½ tsp garlic powder
- 1 tsp ground cumin
- 2 green onions, sliced
- 15g fresh cilantro, chopped
- ½ tsp baking soda
- ½ tsp salt

Directions:
1. Add chickpeas and remaining ingredients into the food processor and process until well combined.
2. Insert a crisper plate in the Tefal air fryer baskets.
3. Make patties from the mixture and place them in both baskets.
4. Select zone 1, then select "air fry" mode and set the temperature to 390 degrees F for 5 minutes. Press "match" to match zone 2 settings to zone 1. Press "start/stop" to begin.

Fried Pickles

Servings: 4
Cooking Time: 15 Minutes
Ingredients:
- 2 cups sliced dill pickles
- 1 cup flour
- 1 tablespoon garlic powder
- 1 tablespoon Cajun spice
- ½ tablespoon cayenne pepper
- Olive Oil or cooking spray

Directions:
1. Mix together the flour and spices in a bowl.
2. Coat the sliced pickles with the flour mixture.
3. Place a crisper plate in each drawer. Put the pickles in a single layer in each drawer. Insert the drawers into the unit.
4. Select zone 1, then AIR FRY, then set the temperature to 400 degrees F/ 200 degrees C with a 15-minute timer. To match zone 2 settings to zone 1, choose MATCH. To begin, select START/STOP.

Nutrition:
- (Per serving) Calories 161 | Fat 4.1g | Sodium 975mg | Carbs 27.5g | Fiber 2.2g | Sugar 1.5g | Protein 4g

Beefy Swiss Pastry

Servings: 4
Cooking Time: 10 Minutes
Ingredients:
- 455g of beef mince
- 70g sliced fresh mushrooms
- 80g chopped onion
- 1-½ teaspoons minced garlic
- ¾ teaspoon dried rosemary, crushed
- ¾ teaspoon paprika
- ½ teaspoon salt
- ¼ teaspoon pepper
- 1 sheet frozen puff pastry, thawed
- 151g refrigerated mashed potatoes
- 100g shredded Swiss cheese
- 1 large egg
- 2 tablespoons water

Directions:
1. Cook the beef, mushrooms, and onion in a large frying pan over medium heat until the meat is no longer pink and the veggies are cooked, 8-10 minutes| crumble the meat.
2. Cook for a further minute after adding the garlic. Drain. Season with salt and pepper. Remove the pan from the heat and set it aside.
3. Roll puff pastry into a rectangle on a lightly floured surface. Make four little rectangles out of the dough.
4. Over each square, spread around 2 teaspoons of potatoes. ¾ cup beef mixture on top of each| 25g cheese on each.
5. In a small bowl, whisk together the egg and water| brush the wash over the pastry edges.
6. Bring opposing pastry corners over each bundle and pinch seams together to seal. Brush with the rest of the egg mixture.
7. Press either "Zone 1" or "Zone 2" and then rotate the knob to select "Air Fry".
8. Set the temperature to 190 degrees C, and then set the time for 5 minutes to preheat.
9. After preheating, spray the Air-Fryer basket with cooking spray and line with parchment paper. Arrange pastry in a single layer and spritz them with cooking spray.
10. Slide the basket into the Air Fryer and set the time for 10 minutes.
11. After that, turn them and again cook for 3 minutes longer.
12. After cooking time is completed, transfer them onto serving plates and serve.

Spinach Patties

Servings: 4
Cooking Time: 10 Minutes
Ingredients:
- 2 large eggs
- 250g frozen spinach, thawed, squeezed dry and chopped
- 185g crumbled feta cheese
- 2 garlic cloves, minced
- ¼ teaspoon pepper
- 1 tube (345g) refrigerated pizza crust

Directions:
1. Whisk eggs in a mixing bowl, reserving 1 tbsp. Combine the spinach, feta cheese, garlic, pepper, and the rest of the beaten eggs in a mixing bowl.
2. Roll out the pizza crust into a 30cm square. Cut each square into four 15cm squares.
3. Place about ⅓ cup of spinach mixture on each square. Fold them into a triangle and pinch them together to seal the edges. Make slits on the top and brush with the remaining egg.
4. Press either "Zone 1" and "Zone 2" and then rotate the knob to select "Air Fry".
5. Set the temperature to 220 degrees C, and then set the time for 5 minutes to preheat.
6. After preheating, spray the Air-Fryer basket with cooking spray and line with parchment paper. Arrange in a single layer and spritz them with cooking spray.
7. Slide the basket into the Air Fryer and set the time for 10 minutes.
8. After cooking time is completed, transfer them onto serving plates and serve.

Crispy Popcorn Shrimp

Servings: 4
Cooking Time: 10 Minutes
Ingredients:
- 170g shrimp, peeled and diced
- ½ cup breadcrumbs
- Salt and black pepper to taste
- 2 eggs, beaten

Directions:
1. Mix breadcrumbs with black pepper and salt in a bowl.
2. Dip the shrimp pieces in the eggs and coat each with breadcrumbs.
3. Divide the shrimp popcorn into the 2 Air Fryer baskets.
4. Return the air fryer basket 1 to Zone 1, and basket 2 to Zone 2 of the Tefal 2-Basket Air Fryer.
5. Choose the "Air Fry" mode for Zone 1 at 400 degrees F and 6 minutes of cooking time.
6. Select the "MATCH COOK" option to copy the settings for Zone 2.
7. Initiate cooking by pressing the START/PAUSE BUTTON.
8. Serve warm.

Five-ingredient Falafel With Garlic-yoghurt Sauce

Servings: 4
Cooking Time: 15 Minutes
Ingredients:
- Falafel:
- 1 (425 g) can chickpeas, drained and rinsed
- 120 ml fresh parsley
- 2 garlic cloves, minced
- ½ tablespoon ground cumin
- 1 tablespoon wholemeal flour
- Salt
- Garlic-Yoghurt Sauce:
- 240 ml non-fat plain Greek yoghurt
- 1 garlic clove, minced
- 1 tablespoon chopped fresh dill
- 2 tablespoons lemon juice

Directions:
1. Make the Falafel: Preheat the air fryer to 180°C. 2. Put the chickpeas into a food processor. Pulse until mostly chopped, then add the parsley, garlic, and cumin and pulse for another 1 to 2 minutes, or until the ingredients are combined and turning into a dough. 3. Add the flour. Pulse a few more times until combined. The dough will have texture, but the chickpeas should be pulsed into small bits. 4. Using clean hands, roll the dough into 8 balls of equal size, then pat the balls down a bit so they are about ½-thick disks. 5. Spray the zone 1 air fryer basket with olive oil cooking spray, then place the falafel patties in the basket in a single layer, making sure they don't touch each other. 6. Fry in the air fryer for 15 minutes. Make the garlic-yoghurt sauce 7. In a small bowl, combine the yoghurt, garlic, dill, and lemon juice. 8. Once the falafel is done cooking and nicely browned on all sides, remove them from the air fryer and season with salt. 9. Serve hot with a side of dipping sauce.

Vegetables And Sides Recipes

Garlic-rosemary Brussels Sprouts

Servings: 4
Cooking Time: 15 Minutes
Ingredients:
- 3 tablespoons olive oil
- 2 garlic cloves, minced
- ½ teaspoon salt
- ¼ teaspoon pepper
- 1-pound Brussels sprouts, trimmed and halved
- ½ cup panko breadcrumbs
- 1½ teaspoons minced fresh rosemary

Directions:
1. Place the first 4 ingredients in a small microwave-safe bowl| microwave on high for 30 seconds.
2. Toss the Brussels sprouts in 2 tablespoons of the microwaved mixture.
3. Place a crisper plate in each drawer. Put the sprouts in a single layer in each drawer. Insert the drawers into the units.
4. Select zone 1, then AIR FRY, then set the temperature to 360 degrees F/ 180 degrees C with a 6-minute timer. To match zone 2 settings to zone 1, choose MATCH. To begin, select START/STOP.
5. Remove the sprouts from the drawers after the timer has finished.
6. Toss the breadcrumbs with the rosemary and remaining oil mixture| sprinkle over the sprouts.
7. Continue cooking until the crumbs are browned, and the sprouts are tender . Serve immediately.

Stuffed Tomatoes

Servings: 2
Cooking Time: 8 Minutes
Ingredients:
- 2 cups brown rice, cooked
- 1 cup tofu, grilled and chopped
- 4 large red tomatoes
- 4 tablespoons basil, chopped
- ¼ tablespoon olive oil
- Salt and black pepper, to taste
- 2 tablespoons lemon juice
- 1 teaspoon red chili powder
- ½ cup Parmesan cheese

Directions:
1. Take a large bowl and mix rice, tofu, basil, olive oil, salt, black pepper, lemon juice, and chili powder.
2. Core the center of the tomatoes.
3. Fill the cavity with the rice mixture.
4. Top them off with the cheese sprinkle.
5. Divide the tomatoes into two air fryer baskets.
6. Turn zone 1 to AIR FRY mode for 8 minutes at 400 degrees F/ 200 degrees C.
7. Select the MATCH button for zone 2.
8. Serve and enjoy.

Rosemary Asparagus & Potatoes

Servings: 6
Cooking Time: 30 Minutes
Ingredients:
- 125g asparagus, trimmed & cut into pieces
- 2 tsp garlic powder
- 2 tbsp rosemary, chopped
- 30ml olive oil
- 679g baby potatoes, quartered
- ½ tsp red pepper flakes
- Pepper
- Salt

Directions:
1. Insert a crisper plate in the Tefal air fryer baskets.
2. Toss potatoes with 1 tablespoon of oil, pepper, and salt in a bowl until well coated.
3. Add potatoes into in zone 1 basket.
4. Toss asparagus with remaining oil, red pepper flakes, pepper, garlic powder, and rosemary in a mixing bowl.
5. Add asparagus into the zone 2 basket.
6. Select zone 1, then select "air fry" mode and set the temperature to 390 degrees F for 20 minutes. Select zone 2, then select "air fry" mode and set the temperature to 390 degrees F for 10 minutes. Press "match" mode, then press "start/stop" to begin.

Nutrition:
- (Per serving) Calories 121 | Fat 5g |Sodium 40mg | Carbs 17.1g | Fiber 4.2g | Sugar 1g | Protein 4g

Bacon Potato Patties

Servings: 2
Cooking Time: 15 Minutes
Ingredients:

- 1 egg
- 600g mashed potatoes
- 119g breadcrumbs
- 2 bacon slices, cooked & chopped
- 235g cheddar cheese, shredded
- 15g flour
- Pepper
- Salt

Directions:
1. In a bowl, mix mashed potatoes with remaining ingredients until well combined.
2. Make patties from potato mixture and place on a plate.
3. Place plate in the refrigerator for 10 minutes
4. Insert a crisper plate in the Tefal air fryer baskets.
5. Place the prepared patties in both baskets.
6. Select zone 1 then select "air fry" mode and set the temperature to 390 degrees F for 15 minutes. Press "match" to match zone 2 settings to zone 1. Press "start/stop" to begin. Turn halfway through.

Nutrition:
- (Per serving) Calories 702 | Fat 26.8g |Sodium 1405mg | Carbs 84.8g | Fiber 2.7g | Sugar 3.8g | Protein 30.5g

Jerk Tofu With Roasted Cabbage

Servings: 4
Cooking Time: 20 Minutes
Ingredients:

- FOR THE JERK TOFU
- 1 (14-ounce) package extra-firm tofu, drained
- 1 tablespoon apple cider vinegar
- 1 tablespoon reduced-sodium soy sauce
- 2 tablespoons jerk seasoning
- Juice of 1 lime
- ½ teaspoon kosher salt
- 2 tablespoons olive oil
- FOR THE CABBAGE
- 1 (14-ounce) bag coleslaw mix
- 1 red bell pepper, thinly sliced
- 2 scallions, thinly sliced
- 2 tablespoons water
- 3 garlic cloves, minced
- ¼ teaspoon fresh thyme leaves
- ¼ teaspoon onion powder
- ¼ teaspoon kosher salt
- ¼ teaspoon freshly ground black pepper

Directions:
1. To prep the jerk tofu: Cut the tofu horizontally into 4 slabs.
2. In a shallow dish (big enough to hold the tofu slabs), whisk together the vinegar, soy sauce, jerk seasoning, lime juice, and salt.
3. Place the tofu in the marinade and turn to coat both sides. Cover and marinate for at least 15 minutes (or up to overnight in the refrigerator).
4. To prep the cabbage: In the Zone 2 basket, combine the coleslaw, bell pepper, scallions, water, garlic, thyme, onion powder, salt, and black pepper.
5. To cook the tofu and cabbage: Install a crisper plate in the Zone 1 basket and add the tofu in a single layer. Brush the tofu with the oil and insert the basket in the unit. Insert the Zone 2 basket in the unit.
6. Select Zone 1, select AIR FRY, set the temperature to 390°F, and set the timer to 15 minutes.
7. Select Zone 2, select ROAST, set the temperature to 330°F, and set the timer to 20 minutes. Select SMART FINISH.
8. Press START/PAUSE to begin cooking.
9. When both timers read 5 minutes, press START/PAUSE. Remove the Zone 1 basket and use silicone-tipped tongs to flip the tofu. Reinsert the basket in the unit. Remove the Zone 2 basket and stir the cabbage. Reinsert the basket and press START/PAUSE to resume cooking.
10. When cooking is complete, the tofu will be crispy and browned around the edges and the cabbage soft.
11. Transfer the tofu to four plates and serve with the cabbage on the side.

Nutrition:
- (Per serving) Calories: 220; Total fat: 12g; Saturated fat: 1.5g; Carbohydrates: 21g; Fiber: 5g; Protein: 12g; Sodium: 817mg

Veggie Burgers With "fried" Onion Rings

Servings: 4
Cooking Time: 25 Minutes
Ingredients:
- FOR THE VEGGIE BURGERS
- 1 (15-ounce) can black beans, drained and rinsed
- ½ cup panko bread crumbs
- 1 large egg
- ¼ cup finely chopped red bell pepper
- ¼ cup frozen corn, thawed
- 1 tablespoon olive oil
- ½ teaspoon garlic powder
- ½ teaspoon ground cumin
- ¼ teaspoon smoked paprika
- Nonstick cooking spray
- 4 hamburger buns
- ¼ cup barbecue sauce, for serving
- FOR THE ONION RINGS
- 1 large sweet onion
- ½ cup all-purpose flour
- 2 large eggs
- 1 cup panko bread crumbs
- ½ teaspoon kosher salt
- Nonstick cooking spray

Directions:
1. To prep the veggie burgers: In a large bowl, mash the beans with a potato masher or a fork. Stir in the panko, egg, bell pepper, corn, oil, garlic powder, cumin, and smoked paprika. Mix well.
2. Shape the mixture into 4 patties. Spritz both sides of each patty with cooking spray.
3. To prep the onion rings: Cut the onion into ½-inch-thick rings.
4. Set up a breading station with three small shallow bowls. Place the flour in the first bowl. In the second bowl, beat the eggs. Place the panko and salt in the third bowl.
5. Bread the onions rings in this order: First, dip them into the flour, coating both sides. Then, dip into the beaten egg. Finally, coat them in the panko. Spritz each with cooking spray.
6. To cook the burgers and onion rings: Install a crisper plate in each of the two baskets. Place 2 veggie burgers in the Zone 1 basket. Place the onion rings in the Zone 2 basket and insert both baskets in the unit.
7. Select Zone 1, select AIR FRY, set the temperature to 390°F, and set the timer to 25 minutes.
8. Select Zone 2, select AIR FRY, set the temperature to 375°F, and set the timer to 10 minutes. Select SMART FINISH.
9. Press START/PAUSE to begin cooking.
10. When the Zone 1 timer reads 10 minutes, press START/PAUSE. Remove the basket and use a silicone spatula to flip the burgers. Reinsert the basket and press START/PAUSE to resume cooking.
11. When the Zone 1 timer reads 10 minutes, press START/PAUSE. Remove the basket and transfer the burgers to a plate. Place the 2 remaining burgers in the basket. Reinsert the basket and press START/PAUSE to resume cooking.
12. When both timers read 5 minutes, press START/PAUSE. Remove the Zone 1 basket and flip the burgers, then reinsert the basket. Remove the Zone 2 basket and shake vigorously to rearrange the onion rings and separate any that have stuck together. Reinsert the basket and press START/PAUSE to resume cooking.
13. When cooking is complete, the veggie burgers should be cooked through and the onion rings golden brown.
14. Place 1 burger on each bun. Top with barbecue sauce and serve with onion rings on the side.

Nutrition:
- (Per serving) Calories: 538; Total fat: 16g; Saturated fat: 2g; Carbohydrates: 83g; Fiber: 10g; Protein: 19g; Sodium: 914mg

Potatoes & Beans

Servings: 4
Cooking Time: 25 Minutes
Ingredients:
- 453g potatoes, cut into pieces
- 15ml olive oil
- 1 tsp garlic powder
- 160g green beans, trimmed
- Pepper
- Salt

Directions:
1. In a bowl, toss green beans, garlic powder, potatoes, oil, pepper, and salt.
2. Insert a crisper plate in the Tefal air fryer baskets.
3. Add green beans and potato mixture to both baskets.
4. Select zone 1 then select "air fry" mode and set the temperature to 380 degrees F for 25 minutes. Press "match" to match zone 2 settings to zone 1. Press "start/stop" to begin. Stir halfway through.

Nutrition:
- (Per serving) Calories 128 | Fat 3.7g | Sodium 49mg | Carbs 22.4g | Fiber 4.7g | Sugar 2.3g | Protein 3.1g

Garlic Potato Wedges In Air Fryer

Servings: 2
Cooking Time: 23 Minutes
Ingredients:
- 4 medium potatoes, peeled and cut into wedges
- 4 tablespoons butter
- 1 teaspoon chopped cilantro
- 1 cup plain flour
- 1 teaspoon garlic, minced
- Salt and black pepper, to taste

Directions:
1. Soak the potato wedges in cold water for about 30 minutes.
2. Drain and pat dry with a paper towel.
3. Boil water in a large pot and boil the wedges for 3 minutes and place on a paper towel.
4. In a bowl, mix garlic, melted butter, salt, pepper, and cilantro.
5. Add the flour to a separate bowl along with the salt and black pepper.
6. Add water to the flour so it gets a runny in texture.
7. Coat the potatoes with the flour mixture and divide them into two foil tins. 8. Place the foil tins in each air fryer basket.
8. Set the zone 1 basket to AIR FRY mode at 390 degrees F/ 200 degrees C for 20 minutes.
9. Select the MATCH button for the zone 2 basket. 11. Once done, serve and enjoy.

Bacon Wrapped Corn Cob

Servings: 4
Cooking Time: 10 Minutes
Ingredients:
- 4 trimmed corns on the cob
- 8 bacon slices

Directions:
1. Wrap the corn cobs with two bacon slices.
2. Place the wrapped cobs into the Tefal 2 Baskets Air Fryer baskets.
3. Return the air fryer basket 1 to Zone 1, and basket 2 to Zone 2 of the Tefal 2-Basket Air Fryer.
4. Choose the "Air Fry" mode for Zone 1 and set the temperature to 355 degrees F and 10 minutes of cooking time.
5. Select the "MATCH COOK" option to copy the settings for Zone 2.
6. Initiate cooking by pressing the START/PAUSE BUTTON.
7. Flip the corn cob once cooked halfway through.
8. Serve warm.

Nutrition:
- (Per serving) Calories 350 | Fat 2.6g |Sodium 358mg | Carbs 64.6g | Fiber 14.4g | Sugar 3.3g | Protein 19.9g

Fried Avocado Tacos

Servings: 4
Cooking Time: 10 Minutes
Ingredients:
- For the sauce:
- 2 cups shredded fresh kale or coleslaw mix
- ¼ cup minced fresh cilantro
- ¼ cup plain Greek yogurt
- 2 tablespoons lime juice
- 1 teaspoon honey
- ¼ teaspoon salt
- ¼ teaspoon ground chipotle pepper
- ¼ teaspoon pepper
- For the tacos:
- 1 large egg, beaten
- ¼ cup cornmeal
- ½ teaspoon salt
- ½ teaspoon garlic powder
- ½ teaspoon ground chipotle pepper
- 2 medium avocados, peeled and sliced
- Cooking spray
- 8 flour tortillas or corn tortillas (6 inches), heated up
- 1 medium tomato, chopped
- Crumbled queso fresco (optional)

Directions:
1. Combine the first 8 ingredients in a bowl. Cover and refrigerate until serving.
2. Place the egg in a shallow bowl. In another shallow bowl, mix the cornmeal, salt, garlic powder, and chipotle pepper.
3. Dip the avocado slices in the egg, then into the cornmeal mixture, gently patting to help adhere.
4. Place a crisper plate in both drawers. Put the avocado slices in the drawers in a single layer. Insert the drawers into the unit.
5. Select zone 1, then AIR FRY, then set the temperature to 360 degrees F/ 180 degrees C with a 6-minute timer. To match zone 2 settings to zone 1, choose MATCH. To begin, select START/STOP.
6. Put the avocado slices, prepared sauce, tomato, and queso fresco in the tortillas and serve.

Acorn Squash Slices

Servings: 6
Cooking Time: 10 Minutes
Ingredients:
- 2 medium acorn squashes
- ⅔ cup packed brown sugar
- ½ cup butter, melted

Directions:
1. Cut the squash in half, remove the seeds and slice into ½ inch slices.
2. Place the squash slices in the air fryer baskets.
3. Drizzle brown sugar and butter over the squash slices.
4. Return the air fryer basket 1 to Zone 1, and basket 2 to Zone 2 of the Tefal 2-Basket Air Fryer.
5. Choose the "Air Fry" mode for Zone 1 and set the temperature to 350 degrees F and 10 minutes of cooking time.
6. Select the "MATCH COOK" option to copy the settings for Zone 2.
7. Initiate cooking by pressing the START/PAUSE BUTTON.
8. Flip the squash once cooked halfway through.
9. Serve.

Nutrition:
- (Per serving) Calories 206 | Fat 3.4g |Sodium 174mg | Carbs 35g | Fiber 9.4g | Sugar 5.9g | Protein 10.6g

Fried Olives

Servings: 6
Cooking Time: 9 Minutes
Ingredients:
- 2 cups blue cheese stuffed olives, drained
- ½ cup all-purpose flour
- 1 cup panko breadcrumbs
- ½ teaspoon garlic powder
- 1 pinch oregano
- 2 eggs

Directions:
1. Mix flour with oregano and garlic powder in a bowl and beat two eggs in another bowl.
2. Spread panko breadcrumbs in a bowl.
3. Coat all the olives with the flour mixture, dip in the eggs and then coat with the panko breadcrumbs.
4. As you coat the olives, place them in the two crisper plates in a single layer, then spray them with cooking oil.
5. Return the crisper plates to the Tefal Dual Zone Air Fryer.
6. Choose the Air Fry mode for Zone 1 and set the temperature to 375 degrees F/ 190 degrees C and the time to 9 minutes.
7. Select the "MATCH" button to copy the settings for Zone 2.
8. Initiate cooking by pressing the START/STOP button.
9. Flip the olives once cooked halfway through, then resume cooking.
10. Serve.

Stuffed Sweet Potatoes

Servings: 4
Cooking Time: 55 Minutes
Ingredients:
- 2 medium sweet potatoes
- 1 teaspoon olive oil
- 1 cup cooked chopped spinach, drained
- 1 cup shredded cheddar cheese, divided
- 2 cooked bacon strips, crumbled
- 1 green onion, chopped
- ¼ cup fresh cranberries, coarsely chopped
- ⅓ cup chopped pecans, toasted
- 2 tablespoons butter
- ¼ teaspoon kosher salt
- ¼ teaspoon pepper

Directions:
1. Brush the sweet potatoes with the oil.
2. Place a crisper plate in both drawers. Add one sweet potato to each drawer. Place the drawers in the unit.
3. Select zone 1, then AIR FRY, then set the temperature to 360 degrees F/ 180 degrees C with a 40-minute timer. To match zone 2 settings to zone 1, choose MATCH. To begin, select START/STOP.
4. Remove the sweet potatoes from the drawers after the timer has finished. Cut them in half lengthwise. Scoop out the pulp, leaving a ¼-inch thick shell. 5. Put the pulp in a large bowl and stir in the spinach, ¾ cup of cheese, bacon, onion, pecans, cranberries, butter, salt, and pepper.
5. Spoon the mixture into the potato shells, mounding the mixture slightly.
6. Place a crisper plate in each drawer. Put one filled potato into each drawer and insert them into the unit.
7. Select zone 1, then AIR FRY, then set the temperature to 360 degrees F/ 180 degrees C with a 10-minute timer. To match zone 2 settings to zone 1, choose MATCH. To begin, select START/STOP.
8. Sprinkle with the remaining ¼ cup of cheese. Cook using the same settings until the cheese is melted .

Air Fryer Vegetables

Servings: 2
Cooking Time: 15 Minutes
Ingredients:
- 1 courgette, diced
- 2 capsicums, diced
- 1 head broccoli, diced
- 1 red onion, diced
- Marinade
- 1 teaspoon smoked paprika
- 1 teaspoon garlic granules
- 1 teaspoon Herb de Provence
- Salt and black pepper, to taste
- 1½ tablespoon olive oil
- 2 tablespoons lemon juice

Directions:
1. Toss the veggies with the rest of the marinade ingredients in a bowl.
2. Spread the veggies in the air fryer baskets.
3. Return the air fryer basket 1 to Zone 1, and basket 2 to Zone 2 of the Tefal 2-Basket Air Fryer.
4. Choose the "Air Fry" mode for Zone 1 at 400 degrees F and 15 minutes of cooking time.
5. Select the "MATCH COOK" option to copy the settings for Zone 2.
6. Initiate cooking by pressing the START/PAUSE BUTTON.
7. Toss the veggies once cooked half way through.
8. Serve warm.

Nutrition:
- (Per serving) Calories 166 | Fat 3.2g |Sodium 437mg | Carbs 28.8g | Fiber 1.8g | Sugar 2.7g | Protein 5.8g

Potato And Parsnip Latkes With Baked Apples

Servings: 4
Cooking Time: 20 Minutes
Ingredients:
- FOR THE LATKES
- 2 medium russet potatoes, peeled
- 1 large egg white
- 2 tablespoons all-purpose flour
- ¼ teaspoon garlic powder
- ¼ teaspoon kosher salt
- ¼ teaspoon freshly ground black pepper
- 1 medium parsnip, peeled and shredded
- 2 scallions, thinly sliced
- 2 tablespoons vegetable oil
- FOR THE BAKED APPLES
- 2 Golden Delicious apples, peeled and diced
- 2 tablespoons granulated sugar
- 2 teaspoons unsalted butter, cut into small pieces

Directions:
1. To prep the latkes: Grate the potatoes using the large holes of a box grater. Squeeze as much liquid out of the potatoes as you can into a large bowl. Set the potatoes aside in a separate bowl.
2. Let the potato liquid sit for 5 minutes, during which time the potato starch will settle to the bottom of the bowl. Pour off the water that has risen to the top, leaving the potato starch in the bowl.
3. Add the egg white, flour, salt, and black pepper to the potato starch to form a thick paste. Add the potatoes, parsnip, and scallions and mix well. Divide the mixture into 4 patties. Brush both sides of each patty with the oil.
4. To prep the baked apples: Place the apples in the Zone 2 basket. Sprinkle the sugar and butter over the top.
5. To cook the latkes and apples: Install a crisper plate in the Zone 1 basket. Place the latkes in the basket in a single layer, then insert the basket in the unit. Insert the Zone 2 basket in the unit.
6. Select Zone 1, select AIR FRY, set the temperature to 375°F, and set the timer to 15 minutes.
7. Select Zone 2, select BAKE, set the temperature to 330°F, and set the timer to 20 minutes. Select SMART FINISH.
8. Press START/PAUSE to begin cooking.
9. When both timers read 5 minutes, press START/PAUSE. Remove the Zone 1 basket and use silicone-tipped tongs or a spatula to flip the latkes. Reinsert the basket in the unit. Remove the Zone 2 basket and gently mash the apples with a fork or the back of a spoon. Reinsert the basket and press START/PAUSE to resume cooking.
10. When cooking is complete, the latkes should be golden brown and cooked through and the apples very soft.
11. Transfer the latkes to a plate and serve with apples on the side.

Nutrition:
- (Per serving) Calories: 257; Total fat: 9g; Saturated fat: 2g; Carbohydrates: 42g; Fiber: 5.5g; Protein: 4g; Sodium: 91mg

Green Tomato Stacks

Servings: 6
Cooking Time: 12 Minutes
Ingredients:
- ¼ cup mayonnaise
- ¼ teaspoon lime zest, grated
- 2 tablespoons lime juice
- 1 teaspoon minced fresh thyme
- ½ teaspoon black pepper
- ¼ cup all-purpose flour
- 2 large egg whites, beaten
- ¾ cup cornmeal
- ¼ teaspoon salt
- 2 medium green tomatoes
- 2 medium re tomatocs
- Cooking spray
- 8 slices Canadian bacon, warmed

Directions:
1. Mix mayonnaise with ¼ teaspoon black pepper, thyme, lime juice and zest in a bowl.
2. Spread flour in one bowl, beat egg whites in another bowl and mix cornmeal with ¼ teaspoon black pepper and salt in a third bowl.
3. Cut the tomatoes into 4 slices and coat each with the flour then dip in the egg whites.
4. Coat the tomatoes slices with the cornmeal mixture.
5. Place the slices in the air fryer baskets.
6. Return the air fryer basket 1 to Zone 1, and basket 2 to Zone 2 of the Tefal 2-Basket Air Fryer.
7. Choose the "Air Fry" mode for Zone 1 at 390 degrees F and 12 minutes of cooking time.
8. Select the "MATCH COOK" option to copy the settings for Zone 2.
9. Initiate cooking by pressing the START/PAUSE BUTTON.
10. Flip the tomatoes once cooked halfway through.
11. Place the green tomato slices on the working surface.
12. Top them with bacon, and red tomato slice.
13. Serve.

Nutrition:
- (Per serving) Calories 113 | Fat 3g | Sodium 152mg | Carbs 20g | Fiber 3g | Sugar 1.1g | Protein 3.5g

Chickpea Fritters

Servings: 6
Cooking Time: 6 Minutes
Ingredients:
- 237ml plain yogurt
- 2 tablespoons sugar
- 1 tablespoon honey
- ½ teaspoon salt
- ½ teaspoon black pepper
- ½ teaspoon crushed red pepper flakes
- 1 can (28g) chickpeas, drained
- 1 teaspoon ground cumin
- ½ teaspoon salt
- ½ teaspoon garlic powder
- ½ teaspoon ground ginger
- 1 large egg
- ½ teaspoon baking soda
- ½ cup fresh coriander, chopped
- 2 green onions, sliced

Directions:
1. Mash chickpeas with rest of the ingredients in a food processor.
2. Layer the two air fryer baskets with a parchment paper.
3. Drop the batter in the baskets spoon by spoon.
4. Return the air fryer basket 1 to Zone 1, and basket 2 to Zone 2 of the Tefal 2-Basket Air Fryer.
5. Choose the "Air Fry" mode for Zone 1 at 400 degrees F and 6 minutes of cooking time.
6. Select the "MATCH COOK" option to copy the settings for Zone 2.
7. Initiate cooking by pressing the START/PAUSE BUTTON.
8. Flip the fritters once cooked halfway through.
9. Serve warm.

Nutrition:
- (Per serving) Calories 284 | Fat 7.9g | Sodium 704mg | Carbs 38.1g | Fiber 1.9g | Sugar 1.9g | Protein 14.8g

Pepper Poppers

Servings: 24
Cooking Time: 20 Minutes
Ingredients:
- 8 ounces cream cheese, softened
- ¾ cup shredded cheddar cheese
- ¾ cup shredded Monterey Jack cheese
- 6 bacon strips, cooked and crumbled
- ¼ teaspoon salt
- ¼ teaspoon garlic powder
- ¼ teaspoon chili powder
- ¼ teaspoon smoked paprika
- 1-pound fresh jalapeño peppers, halved lengthwise and deseeded
- ½ cup dry breadcrumbs
- Sour cream, French onion dip, or ranch salad dressing (optional)

Directions:
1. In a large bowl, combine the cheeses, bacon, and seasonings| mix well. Spoon 1½ to 2 tablespoons of the mixture into each pepper half. Roll them in the breadcrumbs.
2. Place a crisper plate in each drawer. Put the prepared peppers in a single layer in each drawer. Insert the drawers into the unit.
3. Select zone 1, then AIR FRY, then set the temperature to 360 degrees F/ 180 degrees C with a 20-minute timer. To match zone 2 settings to zone 1, choose MATCH. To begin, select START/STOP.
4. Remove the peppers from the drawers after the timer has finished.

Fresh Mix Veggies In Air Fryer

Servings: 4
Cooking Time: 12 Minutes
Ingredients:
- 1 cup cauliflower florets
- 1 cup carrots, peeled chopped
- 1 cup broccoli florets
- 2 tablespoons avocado oil
- Salt, to taste
- ½ teaspoon chili powder
- ½ teaspoon garlic powder
- ½ teaspoon herbs de Provence
- 1 cup Parmesan cheese

Directions:
1. Take a bowl, and add all the veggies to it.
2. Toss and then season the veggies with salt, chili powder, garlic powder, and herbs de Provence.
3. Toss it all well and then drizzle avocado oil.
4. Make sure the ingredients are coated well.
5. Distribute the veggies among both baskets of the air fryer.
6. Turn on the START/STOP button and set it to AIR FRY mode at 390 degrees F/ 200 degrees C for 10-12 minutes.
7. For the zone 2 basket setting, press the MATCH button.
8. After 8 minutes of cooking, press the START/STOP button and then take out the baskets and sprinkle Parmesan cheese on top of the veggies.
9. Then let the cooking cycle complete for the next 3-4 minutes.
10. Once done, serve.

Fried Artichoke Hearts

Servings: 6
Cooking Time: 10 Minutes
Ingredients:
- 3 cans Quartered Artichokes, drained
- ½ cup mayonnaise
- 1 cup panko breadcrumbs
- ⅓ cup grated Parmesan
- salt and black pepper to taste
- Parsley for garnish

Directions:
1. Mix mayonnaise with salt and black pepper and keep the sauce aside.
2. Spread panko breadcrumbs in a bowl.
3. Coat the artichoke pieces with the breadcrumbs.
4. As you coat the artichokes, place them in the two crisper plates in a single layer, then spray them with cooking oil.
5. Return the crisper plates to the Tefal Dual Zone Air Fryer.
6. Choose the Air Fry mode for Zone 1 and set the temperature to 375 degrees F/ 190 degrees C and the time to 10 minutes.
7. Select the "MATCH" button to copy the settings for Zone 2.
8. Initiate cooking by pressing the START/STOP button.
9. Flip the artichokes once cooked halfway through, then resume cooking.
10. Serve warm with mayo sauce.

Buffalo Bites

Servings: 6
Cooking Time: 30 Minutes
Ingredients:
- For the bites:
- 1 small cauliflower head, cut into florets
- 2 tablespoons olive oil
- 3 tablespoons buffalo wing sauce
- 3 tablespoons butter, melted
- For the dip:
- 1½ cups 2% cottage cheese
- ¼ cup fat-free plain Greek yogurt
- ¼ cup crumbled blue cheese
- 1 sachet ranch salad dressing mix
- Celery sticks (optional)

Directions:
1. In a large bowl, combine the cauliflower and oil| toss to coat.
2. Place a crisper plate in each drawer. Put the coated cauliflower florets in each drawer in a single layer. Place the drawers in the unit.
3. Select zone 1, then AIR FRY, then set the temperature to 360 degrees F/ 180 degrees C with a 15-minute timer. To match zone 2 settings to zone 1, choose MATCH. To begin, select START/STOP.
4. Remove the cauliflower from the drawers after the timer has finished.
5. Combine the buffalo sauce and melted butter in a large mixing bowl. Put in the cauliflower and toss to coat. Place on a serving dish and serve.
6. Combine the dip ingredients in a small bowl. Serve with the cauliflower and celery sticks, if desired.

Beef, Pork, And Lamb Recipes

Bo Luc Lac

Servings: 4
Cooking Time: 8 Minutes
Ingredients:
- For the Meat:
- 2 teaspoons soy sauce
- 4 garlic cloves, minced
- 1 teaspoon coarse or flaky salt
- 2 teaspoons sugar
- ¼ teaspoon ground black pepper
- 1 teaspoon toasted sesame oil
- 680 g top rump steak, cut into 1-inch cubes
- Cooking spray
- For the Salad:
- 1 head butterhead lettuce, leaves separated and torn into large pieces
- 60 ml fresh mint leaves
- 120 ml halved baby plum tomatoes
- ½ red onion, halved and thinly sliced
- 2 tablespoons apple cider vinegar
- 1 garlic clove, minced
- 2 teaspoons sugar
- ¼ teaspoon coarse or flaky salt
- ¼ teaspoon ground black pepper
- 2 tablespoons vegetable oil
- For Serving:
- Lime wedges, for garnish
- Coarse salt and freshly cracked black pepper, to taste

Directions:
1. Combine the ingredients for the meat, except for the steak, in a large bowl. Stir to mix well.
2. Dunk the steak cubes in the bowl and press to coat. Wrap the bowl in plastic and marinate under room temperature for at least 30 minutes.
3. Preheat the air fryer to 232°C. Spritz the two air fryer drawers with cooking spray.
4. Discard the marinade and transfer the steak cubes in the two preheated air fryer drawers.
5. Air fry for 4 minutes or until the steak cubes are lightly browned but still have a little pink. Shake the drawers halfway through the cooking time.
6. Meanwhile, combine the ingredients for the salad in a separate large bowl. Toss to mix well.
7. Pour the salad in a large serving bowl and top with the steak cubes. Squeeze the lime wedges over and sprinkle with salt and black pepper before serving.

Steak Fajitas With Onions And Peppers

Servings: 6
Cooking Time: 15 Minutes
Ingredients:
- 1 pound steak
- 1 green bell pepper, sliced
- 1 yellow bell pepper, sliced
- 1 red bell pepper, sliced
- ½ cup sliced white onions
- 1 packet gluten-free fajita seasoning
- Olive oil spray

Directions:
1. Thinly slice the steak against the grain. These should be about ¼-inch slices.
2. Mix the steak with the peppers and onions.
3. Evenly coat with the fajita seasoning.
4. Install a crisper plate in both drawers. Place half the steak mixture in the zone 1 drawer and half in zone 2's, then insert the drawers into the unit.
5. Select zone 1, select AIR FRY, set temperature to 390 degrees F/ 200 degrees C, and set time to 15 minutes. Select MATCH to match zone 2 settings to zone 1. Press the START/STOP button to begin cooking.
6. When the time reaches 10 minutes, press START/STOP to pause the unit. Remove the drawers and flip the steak strips. Re-insert the drawers into the unit and press START/STOP to resume cooking.
7. Serve in warm tortillas.

Nutrition:
- (Per serving) Calories 305 | Fat 17g | Sodium 418mg | Carbs 15g | Fiber 2g | Sugar 4g | Protein 22g

Easy Breaded Pork Chops

Servings: 8
Cooking Time: 20 Minutes
Ingredients:
- 1 egg
- 118ml milk
- 8 pork chops
- 1 packet ranch seasoning
- 238g breadcrumbs
- Pepper
- Salt

Directions:
1. In a small bowl, whisk the egg and milk.
2. In a separate shallow dish, mix breadcrumbs, ranch seasoning, pepper, and salt.
3. Dip each pork chop in the egg mixture, then coat with breadcrumbs.
4. Insert a crisper plate in the Tefal air fryer baskets.
5. Place the coated pork chops in both baskets.
6. Select zone 1, then select air fry mode and set the temperature to 360 degrees F for 12 minutes. Press "match" to match zone 2 settings to zone 1. Press "start/stop" to begin. Turn halfway through.

Mozzarella Stuffed Beef And Pork Meatballs

Servings: 4 To 6
Cooking Time: 12 Minutes
Ingredients:
- 1 tablespoon olive oil
- 1 small onion, finely chopped
- 1 to 2 cloves garlic, minced
- 340 g beef mince
- 340 g pork mince
- 180 ml bread crumbs
- 60 ml grated Parmesan cheese
- 60 ml finely chopped fresh parsley
- ½ teaspoon dried oregano
- 1½ teaspoons salt
- Freshly ground black pepper, to taste
- 2 eggs, lightly beaten
- 140 g low-moisture Mozzarella or other melting cheese, cut into 1-inch cubes

Directions:
1. Preheat a skillet over medium-high heat. Add the oil and cook the onion and garlic until tender, but not browned. 2. Transfer the onion and garlic to a large bowl and add the beef, pork, bread crumbs, Parmesan cheese, parsley, oregano, salt, pepper and eggs. Mix well until all the ingredients are combined. Divide the mixture into 12 evenly sized balls. Make one meatball at a time, by pressing a hole in the meatball mixture with the finger and pushing a piece of Mozzarella cheese into the hole. Mold the meat back into a ball, enclosing the cheese. 3. Preheat the air fryer to 192°C. 4. Transfer meatballs to the two air fryer drawers and air fry for 12 minutes, shaking the drawers and turning the meatballs twice during the cooking process. Serve warm.

Sausage Meatballs

Servings: 24
Cooking Time: 30 Minutes
Ingredients:
- 1 egg, lightly beaten
- 900g pork sausage
- 29g breadcrumbs
- 100g pimientos, drained & diced
- 1 tsp curry powder
- 1 tbsp garlic, minced
- 30ml olive oil
- 1 tbsp fresh rosemary, minced
- 25g parsley, minced
- Pepper
- Salt

Directions:
1. In a bowl, add pork sausage and remaining ingredients and mix until well combined.
2. Insert a crisper plate in the Tefal air fryer baskets.
3. Make small balls from the meat mixture and place them in both baskets.
4. Select zone 1 then select "air fry" mode and set the temperature to 390 degrees F for 10 minutes. Press "match" to match zone 2 settings to zone 1. Press "start/stop" to begin.

Garlic Butter Steaks

Servings: 2
Cooking Time: 25 Minutes
Ingredients:
- 2 (6 ounces each) sirloin steaks or ribeyes
- 2 tablespoons unsalted butter
- 1 clove garlic, crushed
- ½ teaspoon dried parsley
- ½ teaspoon dried rosemary
- Salt and pepper, to taste

Directions:
1. Season the steaks with salt and pepper and set them to rest for about 2 hours before cooking.
2. Put the butter in a bowl. Add the garlic, parsley, and rosemary. Allow the butter to soften.
3. Whip together with a fork or spoon once the butter has softened.
4. When you're ready to cook, install a crisper plate in both drawers. Place the sirloin steaks in a single layer in each drawer. Insert the drawers into the unit.
5. Select zone 1, select AIR FRY, set temperature to 360 degrees F/ 180 degrees C, and set time to 10 minutes. Select MATCH to match zone 2 settings to zone 1. Select START/STOP to begin.
6. Once done, serve with the garlic butter.

Nutrition:
- (Per serving) Calories 519 | Fat 36g | Sodium 245mg | Carbs 1g | Fiber 0g | Sugar 0g | Protein 46g

Steak And Mashed Creamy Potatoes

Servings:1
Cooking Time:45
Ingredients:
- 2 Russet potatoes, peeled and cubed
- ¼ cup butter, divided
- 1/3 cup heavy cream
- ½ cup shredded cheddar cheese
- Salt and black pepper, to taste
- 1 New York strip steak, about a pound
- 1 teaspoon of olive oil
- Oil spray, for greasing

Directions:
1. Rub the potatoes with salt and a little amount of olive oil about a teaspoon.
2. Next, season the steak with salt and black pepper.
3. Place the russet potatoes in a zone 1 basket.
4. Oil spray the steak from both sides and then place it in the zone 2 basket.
5. Set zone 1 to AIR fry mode for 45 minutes at 390 degrees F.
6. Set the zone 2 basket, at 12 minutes at 375 degrees F.
7. Hot start and Lethe Tefale do its magic.
8. One the cooking cycle completes, take out the steak and potatoes.
9. Mash the potatoes and then add butter, heavy cream, and cheese along with salt and black pepper.
10. Serve the mashed potatoes with steak.
11. Enjoy.

Nutrition:
- (Per serving) Calories1932 | Fat 85.2g| Sodium 3069mg | Carbs 82g | Fiber10.3 g| Sugar 5.3g | Protein 22.5g

Tasty Pork Skewers

Servings: 3
Cooking Time: 10 Minutes
Ingredients:
- 450g pork shoulder, cut into ¼-inch pieces
- 66ml soy sauce
- ½ tbsp garlic, crushed
- 1 tbsp ginger paste
- 1 ½ tsp sesame oil
- 22ml rice vinegar
- 21ml honey
- Pepper
- Salt

Directions:
1. In a bowl, mix meat with the remaining ingredients. Cover and place in the refrigerator for 30 minutes.
2. Thread the marinated meat onto the soaked skewers.
3. Insert a crisper plate in the Tefal air fryer baskets.
4. Place the pork skewers in both baskets.
5. Select zone 1, then select "air fry" mode and set the temperature to 360 degrees F for 10 minutes. Press "match" and then press "start/stop" to begin. Turn halfway through.

Air Fryer Meatloaves

Servings: 4
Cooking Time: 22 Minutes.
Ingredients:
- ⅓ cup milk
- 2 tablespoons basil pesto
- 1 egg, beaten
- 1 garlic clove, minced
- ¼ teaspoons black pepper
- 1 lb. ground beef
- ⅓ cup panko bread crumbs
- 8 pepperoni slices
- ½ cup marinara sauce, warmed
- 1 tablespoon fresh basil, chopped

Directions:
1. Mix pesto, milk, egg, garlic, and black pepper in a medium-sized bowl.
2. Stir in ground beef and bread crumbs, then mix.
3. Make the 4 small-sized loaves with this mixture and top them with 2 pepperoni slices.
4. Press the slices into the meatloaves.
5. Place the meatloaves in the two crisper plates.
6. Return the crisper plate to the Tefal Dual Zone Air Fryer.
7. Choose the Air Fry mode for Zone 1 and set the temperature to 390 degrees F and the time to 22 minutes.
8. Select the "MATCH" button to copy the settings for Zone 2.
9. Initiate cooking by pressing the START/STOP button.
10. Top them with marinara sauce and basil to serve.
11. Serve warm.

Nutrition:
- (Per serving) Calories 316 | Fat 12.2g |Sodium 587mg | Carbs 12.2g | Fiber 1g | Sugar 1.8g | Protein 25.8g

Sausage And Pork Meatballs

Servings: 8
Cooking Time: 8 To 12 Minutes
Ingredients:
- 1 large egg
- 1 teaspoon gelatin
- 450 g pork mince
- 230 g Italian-seasoned sausage, casings removed, crumbled
- 80 ml Parmesan cheese
- 60 ml finely diced onion
- 1 tablespoon tomato paste
- 1 teaspoon minced garlic
- 1 teaspoon dried oregano
- ¼ teaspoon red pepper flakes
- Sea salt and freshly ground black pepper, to taste
- Keto-friendly marinara sauce, for serving

Directions:
1. Beat the egg in a small bowl and sprinkle with the gelatin. Allow to sit for 5 minutes.
2. In a large bowl, combine the pork mince, sausage, Parmesan, onion, tomato paste, garlic, oregano, and red pepper flakes. Season with salt and black pepper.
3. Stir the gelatin mixture, then add it to the other ingredients and, using clean hands, mix to ensure that everything is well combined. Form into 1½-inch round meatballs.
4. Set the air fryer to 204ºC. Place the meatballs in the two air fryer drawers in a single layer. Air fry for 5 minutes. Flip and cook for 3 to 7 minutes more, or until an instant-read thermometer reads 72ºC.

Tomahawk Steak

Servings: 4
Cooking Time: 12 Minutes
Ingredients:
- 4 tablespoons butter, softened
- 2 cloves garlic, minced
- 2 teaspoons chopped fresh parsley
- 1 teaspoon chopped chives
- 1 teaspoon chopped fresh thyme
- 1 teaspoon chopped fresh rosemary
- 2 (2 pounds each) bone-in ribeye steaks
- Kosher salt, to taste
- Freshly ground black pepper, to taste

Directions:
1. In a small bowl, combine the butter and herbs. Place the mixture in the center of a piece of plastic wrap and roll it into a log. Twist the ends together to keep it tight and refrigerate until hardened, about 20 minutes.
2. Season the steaks on both sides with salt and pepper.
3. Install a crisper plate in both drawers. Place one steak in the zone 1 drawer and one in zone 2's, then insert the drawers into the unit.
4. Select zone 1, select AIR FRY, set temperature to 390 degrees F/ 200 degrees C, and set time to 12 minutes. Select MATCH to match zone 2 settings to zone 1. Press the START/STOP button to begin cooking.
5. When the time reaches 10 minutes, press START/STOP to pause the unit. Remove the drawers and flip the steaks. Add the herb-butter to the tops of the steaks. Re-insert the drawers into the unit and press START/STOP to resume cooking.
6. Serve and enjoy!

Nutrition:
- (Per serving) Calories 338 | Fat 21.2g | Sodium 1503mg | Carbs 5.1g | Fiber 0.3g | Sugar 4.6g | Protein 29.3g

Simple Beef Sirloin Roast

Servings: 16
Cooking Time: 50 Minutes
Ingredients:
- 2 (2½-pound) sirloin roast
- Salt and ground black pepper, as required

Directions:
1. Grease each basket of "Zone 1" and "Zone 2" of Tefal 2-Basket Air Fryer.
2. Press "Zone 1" and "Zone 2" and then rotate the knob for each zone to select "Roast".
3. Set the temperature to 350 degrees F/ 175 degrees C for both zones and then set the time for 5 minutes to preheat.
4. Rub ach roast with salt and black pepper generously.
5. After preheating, arrange 1 roast into the basket of each zone.
6. Slide each basket into Air Fryer and set the time for 50 minutes.
7. After cooking time is completed, remove each roast from Air Fryer and place onto a platter for about 10 minutes before slicing.
8. With a sharp knife, cut each roast into desired-sized slices and serve.

Pork Chops With Apples

Servings: 2
Cooking Time: 20 Minutes
Ingredients:
- ½ small red cabbage, sliced
- 1 apple, sliced
- 1 sweet onion, sliced
- 2 tablespoons oil
- ½ teaspoon cumin
- ½ teaspoon paprika
- Salt and black pepper, to taste
- 2 boneless pork chops (1″ thick)

Directions:
1. Toss pork chops with apple and the rest of the ingredients in a bowl.
2. Divide the mixture in the air fryer baskets.
3. Return the air fryer basket 1 to Zone 1, and basket 2 to Zone 2 of the Tefal 2-Basket Air Fryer.
4. Choose the "Air Fry" mode for Zone 1 and set the temperature to 400 degrees F and 15 minutes of cooking time.
5. Select the "MATCH COOK" option to copy the settings for Zone 2.
6. Initiate cooking by pressing the START/PAUSE BUTTON.
7. Serve warm.

Five-spice Pork Belly

Servings: 4
Cooking Time: 17 Minutes
Ingredients:
- 450 g unsalted pork belly
- 2 teaspoons Chinese five-spice powder
- Sauce:
- 1 tablespoon coconut oil
- 1 (1-inch) piece fresh ginger, peeled and grated
- 2 cloves garlic, minced
- 120 ml beef or chicken stock
- ¼ to 120 ml liquid or powdered sweetener
- 3 tablespoons wheat-free tamari
- 1 spring onion, sliced, plus more for garnish

Directions:
1. Spray the two air fryer drawers with avocado oil. Preheat the air fryer to 204°C. 2. Cut the pork belly into ½-inch-thick slices and season well on all sides with the five-spice powder. Place the slices in a single layer in the two air fryer drawers and cook for 8 minutes, or until cooked to your liking, flipping halfway through. 3. While the pork belly cooks, make the sauce: Heat the coconut oil in a small saucepan over medium heat. Add the ginger and garlic and sauté for 1 minute, or until fragrant. Add the stock, sweetener, and tamari and simmer for 10 to 15 minutes, until thickened. Add the spring onion and cook for another minute, until the spring onion is softened. Taste and adjust the seasoning to your liking. 4. Transfer the pork belly to a large bowl. Pour the sauce over the pork belly and coat well. Place the pork belly slices on a serving platter and garnish with sliced spring onions. 5. Best served fresh. Store leftovers in an airtight container in the fridge for up to 4 days. Reheat in a preheated 204°C air fryer for 3 minutes, or until heated through.

Cheeseburgers With Barbecue Potato Chips

Servings: 4
Cooking Time: 15 Minutes
Ingredients:
- FOR THE CHEESEBURGERS
- 1 pound ground beef (85 percent lean)
- ¼ teaspoon kosher salt
- ¼ teaspoon freshly ground black pepper
- ½ teaspoon olive oil
- 4 slices American cheese
- 4 hamburger rolls
- FOR THE POTATO CHIPS
- 2 large russet potatoes
- 2 teaspoons vegetable oil
- 1½ teaspoons smoked paprika
- 1 teaspoon light brown sugar
- ½ teaspoon garlic powder
- ½ teaspoon kosher salt
- ¼ teaspoon chili powder

Directions:
1. To prep the cheeseburgers: Season the beef with the salt and black pepper. Form the beef into 4 patties about 1 inch thick. Brush both sides of the beef patties with the oil.
2. To prep the potato chips: Fill a large bowl with ice water. Using a mandoline or sharp knife, cut the potatoes into very thin (⅛- to 1/16-inch) slices. Soak the potatoes in the ice water for 30 minutes.
3. Drain the potatoes and pat dry with a paper towel. Place in a large bowl and toss with the oil, smoked paprika, brown sugar, garlic powder, salt, and chili powder.
4. To cook the cheeseburgers and potato chips: Install a crisper plate in each of the two baskets. Place the burgers in the Zone 1 basket and insert the basket in the unit. Place the potato slices in the Zone 2 basket and insert the basket in the unit.
5. Select Zone 1, select AIR FRY, set the temperature to 390°F, and set the time to 12 minutes.
6. Select Zone 2, select AIR FRY, set the temperature to 390°F, and set the time to 15 minutes. Select SMART FINISH.
7. Press START/PAUSE to begin cooking.
8. At 5-minute intervals, press START/PAUSE. Remove the Zone 2 basket and shake the potato chips to keep them from sticking to each other. Reinsert the basket and press START/PAUSE to resume cooking.
9. When cooking is complete, the burgers should be cooked to your preferred doneness and the potato chips should be crisp and golden brown.
10. Top each burger patty in the basket with a slice of cheese. Turn the air fryer off and let the cheese melt inside the unit, or cover the basket with aluminum foil and let stand for 1 to 2 minutes, until the cheese is melted. Serve the cheeseburgers on buns with the chips on the side.

Nutrition:
- (Per serving) Calories: 475; Total fat: 22g; Saturated fat: 8g; Carbohydrates: 38g; Fiber: 2g; Protein: 32g; Sodium: 733mg

Tender Pork Chops

Servings: 2
Cooking Time: 20 Minutes
Ingredients:
- 2 pork chops
- 1 tsp dry mustard
- 1 tsp ground coriander
- 1 tbsp chilli powder
- 30ml olive oil
- ¼ tsp cayenne
- ½ tsp ground cumin
- 1 tsp smoked paprika
- Pepper
- Salt

Directions:
1. In a small bowl, mix chilli powder, paprika, cayenne, coriander, mustard, pepper, and salt.
2. Brush the pork chops with oil and rub with spice mixture.
3. Insert a crisper plate in the Tefal air fryer baskets.
4. Place the chops in both baskets.
5. Select zone 1, then select "air fry" mode and set the temperature to 375 degrees F for 10 minutes. Press "match" to match zone 2 settings to zone 1. Press "start/stop" to begin. Turn halfway through.

Barbecue Ribs With Roasted Green Beans And Shallots

Servings: 4
Cooking Time: 40 Minutes
Ingredients:
- FOR THE RIBS
- 1 tablespoon light brown sugar
- 1 tablespoon smoked paprika
- 1 tablespoon chili powder
- 2 teaspoons kosher salt
- 1 teaspoon freshly ground black pepper
- 1 teaspoon garlic powder
- ¼ teaspoon cayenne pepper (optional)
- 2 pounds pork ribs
- 1 cup barbecue sauce (your favorite), for serving
- FOR THE GREEN BEANS AND SHALLOTS
- 1 pound green beans, trimmed
- 2 shallots, sliced
- 1 tablespoon olive oil
- ¼ teaspoon kosher salt

Directions:
1. To prep the ribs: In a small bowl, combine the brown sugar, paprika, chili powder, salt, black pepper, garlic powder, and cayenne (if using).
2. Rub the spice blend all over both sides of the ribs.
3. To prep the green beans and shallots: In a large bowl, combine the green beans, shallots, and oil. Toss to coat. Season with the salt.
4. To cook the ribs and vegetables: Install a crisper plate in each of the two baskets. Place the ribs in the Zone 1 basket and insert the basket in the unit. Place the green beans in the Zone 2 basket and insert the basket in the unit.
5. Select Zone 1, select AIR FRY, set the temperature to 375°F, and set the time to 40 minutes.
6. Select Zone 2, select ROAST, set the temperature to 400°F, and set the time to 20 minutes. Select SMART FINISH.
7. Press START/PAUSE to begin cooking.
8. When the Zone 1 timer reads 10 minutes, press START/PAUSE. Increase the temperature of Zone 1 to 400°F. Press START/PAUSE to resume cooking.
9. When cooking is complete, an instant-read thermometer inserted into the ribs should read 170°F and the green beans should be tender-crisp. Serve topped with your favorite barbecue sauce.

Nutrition:
- (Per serving) Calories: 541; Total fat: 27g; Saturated fat: 9g; Carbohydrates: 48g; Fiber: 4.5g; Protein: 28g; Sodium: 1,291mg

Seasoned Flank Steak

Servings: 12
Cooking Time: 30 Minutes
Ingredients:
- 2 (2-pound) flank steaks
- 3 tablespoons taco seasoning rub

Directions:
1. Grease each basket of "Zone 1" and "Zone 2" of Tefal 2-Basket Air Fryer.
2. Press "Zone 1" and "Zone 2" and then rotate the knob for each zone to select "Bake".
3. Set the temperature to 420 degrees F/ 215 degrees C for both zones and then set the time for 5 minutes to preheat.
4. Rub the steaks with taco seasoning evenly.
5. After preheating, arrange 1 steak into the basket of each zone.
6. Slide each basket into Air Fryer and set the time for 30 minutes.
7. After cooking time is completed, remove the steaks from Air Fryer and place onto a cutting board for about 10-15 minutes before slicing.
8. With a sharp knife, cut each steak into desired size slices and serve.

Tasty Lamb Patties

Servings: 8
Cooking Time: 12 Minutes
Ingredients:
- 900g ground lamb
- 1 tbsp ground coriander
- 4g fresh parsley, chopped
- 1 tsp garlic, minced
- ½ tsp cinnamon
- 1 tsp paprika
- 1 tbsp ground cumin
- Pepper
- Salt

Directions:
1. Add ground meat and remaining ingredients into a bowl and mix until well combined.
2. Insert a crisper plate in the Tefal air fryer baskets.
3. Make patties from the meat mixture and place in both baskets.
4. Select zone 1, then select "air fry" mode and set the temperature to 390 degrees F for 12 minutes. Press "match" to match zone 2 settings to zone 1. Press "start/stop" to begin. Turn halfway through.

Italian Sausages With Peppers And Teriyaki Rump Steak With Broccoli

Servings: 7
Cooking Time: 28 Minutes
Ingredients:
- Italian Sausages with Peppers:
- 1 medium onion, thinly sliced
- 1 yellow or orange pepper, thinly sliced
- 1 red pepper, thinly sliced
- 60 ml avocado oil or melted coconut oil
- 1 teaspoon fine sea salt
- 6 Italian-seasoned sausages
- Dijon mustard, for serving (optional)
- Teriyaki Rump Steak with Broccoli:
- 230 g rump steak
- 80 ml teriyaki marinade
- 1½ teaspoons sesame oil
- ½ head broccoli, cut into florets
- 2 red peppers, sliced
- Fine sea salt and ground black pepper, to taste
- Cooking spray

Directions:
1. Make the Italian Sausages with Peppers :
2. Preheat the air fryer to 204°C.
3. Place the onion and peppers in a large bowl. Drizzle with the oil and toss well to coat the veggies. Season with the salt.
4. Place the onion and peppers in a pie pan and cook in the air fryer for 8 minutes, stirring halfway through. Remove from the air fryer and set aside.
5. Spray the zone 1 air fryer drawer with avocado oil. Place the sausages in the zone 1 air fryer drawer and air fry for 20 minutes, or until crispy and golden brown. During the last minute or two of cooking, add the onion and peppers to the drawer with the sausages to warm them through.
6. Place the onion and peppers on a serving platter and arrange the sausages on top. Serve Dijon mustard on the side, if desired.
7. Store leftovers in an airtight container in the fridge for up to 7 days or in the freezer for up to a month. Reheat in a preheated 200°C air fryer for 3 minutes, or until heated through.
8. Make the Teriyaki Rump Steak with Broccoli :
9. Toss the rump steak in a large bowl with teriyaki marinade. Wrap the bowl in plastic and refrigerate to marinate for at least an hour.
10. Preheat the air fryer to 204°C and spritz with cooking spray.
11. Discard the marinade and transfer the steak in the preheated zone 2 air fryer drawer. Spritz with cooking spray.
12. Air fry for 13 minutes or until well browned. Flip the steak halfway through.
13. Meanwhile, heat the sesame oil in a nonstick skillet over medium heat. Add the broccoli and red pepper. Sprinkle with salt and ground black pepper. Sauté for 5 minutes or until the broccoli is tender.
14. Transfer the air fried rump steak on a plate and top with the sautéed broccoli and pepper. Serve hot.

Roast Souvlaki-style Pork With Lemon-feta Baby Potatoes

Servings: 4
Cooking Time: 40 Minutes
Ingredients:
- FOR THE PORK
- 1½ pounds pork tenderloin, cut into bite-size cubes
- ¼ cup olive oil
- ¼ cup fresh lemon juice
- 2 teaspoons minced garlic
- 2 teaspoons honey
- 1½ teaspoons dried oregano
- ¼ teaspoon kosher salt
- ¼ teaspoon freshly ground black pepper
- FOR THE POTATOES
- 1 pound baby red or yellow potatoes, halved
- 1 tablespoon olive oil
- Grated zest and juice of 1 lemon
- ½ teaspoon kosher salt
- ¼ teaspoon freshly ground black pepper
- ⅓ cup crumbled feta cheese
- 2 tablespoons chopped fresh parsley

Directions:
1. To prep the pork: In a large bowl, combine the pork, oil, lemon juice, garlic, honey, oregano, salt, and black pepper. If desired, cover and refrigerate up to 24 hours.
2. To prep the potatoes: In a large bowl, combine the potatoes, oil, lemon zest, lemon juice, salt, and black pepper. Mix to coat the potatoes.
3. To cook the pork and potatoes: Install a crisper plate in each of the two baskets. Place the pork in the Zone 1 basket and insert the basket in the unit. Place the potatoes in the Zone 2 basket and insert the basket in the unit.
4. Select Zone 1, select ROAST, set the temperature to 390°F, and set the time to 20 minutes.
5. Select Zone 2, select AIR FRY, set the temperature to 400°F, and set the time to 40 minutes. Select SMART FINISH.
6. Press START/PAUSE to begin cooking.
7. When cooking is complete, the pork will be cooked through (an instant-read thermometer should read 145°F) and the potatoes will be tender and beginning to brown around the edges.
8. Stir the feta and parsley into the potatoes. Serve the pork and potatoes while hot.

Nutrition:
- (Per serving) Calories: 395; Total fat: 17g; Saturated fat: 4.5g; Carbohydrates: 24g; Fiber: 2g; Protein: 37g; Sodium: 399mg

Paprika Pork Chops

Servings: 4
Cooking Time: 12 Minutes
Ingredients:
- 4 bone-in pork chops (6–8 ounces each)
- 1½ tablespoons brown sugar
- 1¼ teaspoons kosher salt
- 1 teaspoon dried Italian seasoning
- 1 teaspoon smoked paprika
- ¼ teaspoon garlic powder
- ¼ teaspoon onion powder
- ¼ teaspoon black pepper
- 1 teaspoon sweet paprika
- 3 tablespoons butter, melted
- 2 tablespoons chopped fresh parsley
- Cooking spray

Directions:
1. In a small mixing bowl, combine the brown sugar, salt, Italian seasoning, smoked paprika, garlic powder, onion powder, black pepper, and sweet paprika. Mix thoroughly.
2. Brush the pork chops on both sides with the melted butter.
3. Rub the spice mixture all over the meat on both sides.
4. Install a crisper plate in both drawers. Place half the chops in the zone 1 drawer and half in zone 2's, then insert the drawers into the unit.
5. Select zone 1, select AIR FRY, set temperature to 390 degrees F/ 200 degrees C, and set time to 12 minutes. Select MATCH to match zone 2 settings to zone 1. Press the START/STOP button to begin cooking.
6. When the time reaches 10 minutes, press START/STOP to pause the unit. Remove the drawers and flip the chops. Re-insert the drawers into the unit and press START/STOP to resume cooking.
7. Serve and enjoy!

Nutrition:
- (Per serving) Calories 338 | Fat 21.2g | Sodium 1503mg | Carbs 5.1g | Fiber 0.3g | Sugar 4.6g | Protein 29.3g

Beef And Bean Taquitos With Mexican Rice

Servings: 4
Cooking Time: 15 Minutes
Ingredients:
- FOR THE TAQUITOS
- ½ pound ground beef (85 percent lean)
- 1 tablespoon taco seasoning
- 8 (6-inch) soft white corn tortillas
- Nonstick cooking spray
- ¾ cup canned refried beans
- ½ cup shredded Mexican blend cheese (optional)
- FOR THE MEXICAN RICE
- 1 cup dried instant white rice (not microwavable)
- 1½ cups chicken broth
- ¼ cup jarred salsa
- 2 tablespoons canned tomato sauce
- 1 tablespoon vegetable oil
- ½ teaspoon kosher salt

Directions:
1. To prep the taquitos: In a large bowl, mix the ground beef and taco seasoning until well combined.
2. Mist both sides of each tortilla lightly with cooking spray.
3. To prep the Mexican rice: In the Zone 2 basket, combine the rice, broth, salsa, tomato sauce, oil, and salt. Stir well to ensure all of the rice is submerged in the liquid.
4. To cook the taquitos and rice: Install a crisper plate in the Zone 1 basket. Place the seasoned beef in the basket and insert the basket in the unit. Insert the Zone 2 basket in the unit.
5. Select Zone 1, select AIR FRY, set the temperature to 390°F, and set the time to 15 minutes.
6. Select Zone 2, select BAKE, set the temperature to 350°F, and set the time to 10 minutes. Select SMART FINISH.
7. Press START/PAUSE to begin cooking.
8. When the Zone 1 timer reads 10 minutes, press START/PAUSE. Remove the basket and transfer the beef to a medium bowl. Add the refried beans and cheese (if using) and combine well. Spoon 2 tablespoons of the filling onto each tortilla and roll tightly. Place the taquitos in the Zone 1 basket seam-side down. Reinsert the basket in the unit and press START/PAUSE to resume cooking.
9. When cooking is complete, the taquitos should be crisp and golden brown and the rice cooked through. Serve hot.

Nutrition:
- (Per serving) Calories: 431; Total fat: 18g; Saturated fat: 4g; Carbohydrates: 52g; Fiber: 5.5g; Protein: 18g; Sodium: 923mg

Turkey And Beef Meatballs

Servings: 6
Cooking Time: 24 Minutes.
Ingredients:
- 1 medium shallot, minced
- 2 tablespoons olive oil
- 3 garlic cloves, minced
- ¼ cup panko crumbs
- 2 tablespoons whole milk
- ⅔ lb. lean ground beef
- ⅓ lb. bulk turkey sausage
- 1 large egg, lightly beaten
- ¼ cup parsley, chopped
- 1 tablespoon fresh thyme, chopped
- 1 tablespoon fresh rosemary, chopped
- 1 tablespoon Dijon mustard
- ½ teaspoon salt

Directions:
1. Preheat your oven to 400 degrees F. Place a medium non-stick pan over medium-high heat.
2. Add oil and shallot, then sauté for 2 minutes.
3. Toss in the garlic and cook for 1 minute.
4. Remove this pan from the heat.
5. Whisk panko with milk in a large bowl and leave it for 5 minutes.
6. Add cooked shallot mixture and mix well.
7. Stir in egg, parsley, turkey sausage, beef, thyme, rosemary, salt, and mustard.
8. Mix well, then divide the mixture into 1 ½-inch balls.
9. Divide these balls into the two crisper plates and spray them with cooking oil.
10. Return the crisper plates to the Tefal Dual Zone Air Fryer.
11. Choose the Air Fry mode for Zone 1 and set the temperature to 400 degrees F and the time to 21 minutes.
12. Select the "MATCH" button to copy the settings for Zone 2.
13. Initiate cooking by pressing the START/STOP button.
14. Serve warm.

Nutrition:
- (Per serving) Calories 551 | Fat 31g |Sodium 1329mg | Carbs 1.5g | Fiber 0.8g | Sugar 0.4g | Protein 64g

Panko Crusted Calf's Liver Strips

Servings: 4
Cooking Time: 23 To 25 Minutes
Ingredients:
- 450 g sliced calf's liver, cut into ½-inch wide strips
- 2 eggs
- 2 tablespoons milk
- 120 ml whole wheat flour
- 475 ml panko breadcrumbs
- Salt and ground black pepper, to taste
- Cooking spray

Directions:
1. Preheat the air fryer to 200°C and spritz with cooking spray.
2. Rub the calf's liver strips with salt and ground black pepper on a clean work surface.
3. Whisk the eggs with milk in a large bowl. Pour the flour in a shallow dish. Pour the panko on a separate shallow dish.
4. Dunk the liver strips in the flour, then in the egg mixture. Shake the excess off and roll the strips over the panko to coat well.
5. Arrange the liver strips in a single layer in the two preheated air fryer drawers and spritz with cooking spray.
6. Air fry for 5 minutes or until browned. Flip the strips halfway through.
7. Serve immediately.

Bacon-wrapped Hot Dogs With Mayo-ketchup Sauce

Servings: 5
Cooking Time: 10 To 12 Minutes
Ingredients:
- 10 thin slices of bacon
- 5 pork hot dogs, halved
- 1 teaspoon cayenne pepper
- Sauce:
- 60 ml mayonnaise
- 4 tablespoons ketchup
- 1 teaspoon rice vinegar
- 1 teaspoon chili powder

Directions:
1. Preheat the air fryer to 200°C. 2. Arrange the slices of bacon on a clean work surface. One by one, place the halved hot dog on one end of each slice, season with cayenne pepper and wrap the hot dog with the bacon slices and secure with toothpicks as needed. 3. Place half the wrapped hot dogs in the two air fryer drawers and air fry for 10 to 12 minutes or until the bacon becomes browned and crispy. 4. Make the sauce: Stir all the ingredients for the sauce in a small bowl. Wrap the bowl in plastic and set in the refrigerator until ready to serve. 5. Transfer the hot dogs to a platter and serve hot with the sauce.

Meatloaf

Servings: 6
Cooking Time: 25 Minutes
Ingredients:
- For the meatloaf:
- 2 pounds ground beef
- 2 eggs, beaten
- 2 cups old-fashioned oats, regular or gluten-free
- ½ cup evaporated milk
- ½ cup chopped onion
- ½ teaspoon garlic salt
- For the sauce:
- 1 cup ketchup
- ¾ cup brown sugar, packed
- ¼ cup chopped onion
- ½ teaspoon liquid smoke
- ¼ teaspoon garlic powder
- Olive oil cooking spray

Directions:
1. In a large bowl, combine all the meatloaf ingredients.
2. Spray 2 sheets of foil with olive oil cooking spray.
3. Form the meatloaf mixture into a loaf shape, cut in half, and place each half on one piece of foil.
4. Roll the foil up a bit on the sides. Allow it to be slightly open.
5. Put all the sauce ingredients in a saucepan and whisk until combined on medium-low heat. This should only take 1–2 minutes
6. Install a crisper plate in both drawers. Place half the meatloaf in the zone 1 drawer and half in zone 2's, then insert the drawers into the unit.
7. Select zone 1, select AIR FRY, set temperature to 390 degrees F/ 200 degrees C, and set time to 25 minutes. Select MATCH to match zone 2 settings to zone 1. Press the START/STOP button to begin cooking.
8. When the time reaches 20 minutes, press START/STOP to pause the unit. Remove the drawers and coat the meatloaf with the sauce using a brush. Re-insert the drawers into the unit and press START/STOP to resume cooking.
9. Carefully remove and serve.

Nutrition:
- (Per serving) Calories 727 | Fat 34g | Sodium 688mg | Carbs 57g | Fiber 3g | Sugar 34g | Protein 49g

Air Fryer Chicken-fried Steak

Servings: 4
Cooking Time: 20 Minutes
Ingredients:
- 450 g beef braising steak
- 700 ml low-fat milk, divided
- 1 teaspoon dried thyme
- 1 teaspoon dried rosemary
- 2 medium egg whites
- 235 ml gluten-free breadcrumbs
- 120 ml coconut flour
- 1 tablespoon Cajun seasoning

Directions:
1. In a bowl, marinate the steak in 475 ml of milk for 30 to 45 minutes.
2. Remove the steak from milk, shake off the excess liquid, and season with the thyme and rosemary. Discard the milk.
3. In a shallow bowl, beat the egg whites with the remaining 235 ml of milk.
4. In a separate shallow bowl, combine the breadcrumbs, coconut flour, and seasoning.
5. Dip the steak in the egg white mixture then dredge in the breadcrumb mixture, coating well.
6. Place the steak in the zone 1 drawer of an air fryer.
7. Set the temperature to 200°C, close, and cook for 10 minutes.
8. Open the air fryer, turn the steaks, close, and cook for 10 minutes. Let rest for 5 minutes.

Balsamic Steak Tips With Roasted Asparagus And Mushroom Medley

Servings: 4
Cooking Time: 25 Minutes
Ingredients:
- FOR THE STEAK TIPS
- 1½ pounds sirloin tips
- ½ cup olive oil
- ¼ cup balsamic vinegar
- ¼ cup packed light brown sugar
- 1 tablespoon reduced-sodium soy sauce
- 1 teaspoon finely chopped fresh rosemary
- 1 teaspoon minced garlic
- FOR THE ASPARAGUS AND MUSHROOMS
- 6 ounces sliced cremini mushrooms
- 1 small red onion, sliced
- 1 tablespoon olive oil
- 1 pound asparagus, tough ends trimmed
- ⅛ teaspoon kosher salt

Directions:
1. To prep the steak tips: In a large bowl, combine the sirloin tips, oil, vinegar, brown sugar, soy sauce, rosemary, and garlic. Mix well to coat the steak.
2. To prep the mushrooms: In a large bowl, combine the mushrooms, onion, and oil.
3. To cook the steak and vegetables: Install a crisper plate in each of the two baskets. Shake any excess marinade from the steak tips, place the steak in the Zone 1 basket, and insert the basket in the unit. Place the mushrooms and onions in the Zone 2 basket and insert the basket in the unit.
4. Select Zone 1, select AIR FRY, set the temperature to 400°F, and set the time to 12 minutes.
5. Select Zone 2, select ROAST, set the temperature to 400°F, and set the time to 25 minutes. Select SMART FINISH.
6. Press START/PAUSE to begin cooking.
7. When the Zone 2 timer reads 10 minutes, press START/PAUSE. Remove the basket, add the asparagus to the mushrooms and onion, and sprinkle with salt. Reinsert the basket and press START/PAUSE to resume cooking.
8. When cooking is complete, the beef should be cooked to your liking and the asparagus crisp-tender. Serve warm.

Nutrition:
- (Per serving) Calories: 524; Total fat: 33g; Saturated fat: 2.5g; Carbohydrates: 16g; Fiber: 3g; Protein: 41g; Sodium: 192mg

Cinnamon-beef Kofta

Servings: 12 Koftas
Cooking Time: 13 Minutes
Ingredients:
- 680 g lean beef mince
- 1 teaspoon onion granules
- ¾ teaspoon ground cinnamon
- ¾ teaspoon ground dried turmeric
- 1 teaspoon ground cumin
- ¾ teaspoon salt
- ¼ teaspoon cayenne
- 12 (3½- to 4-inch-long) cinnamon sticks
- Cooking spray

Directions:
1. Preheat the air fryer to 192°C. Spritz the two air fryer drawers with cooking spray.
2. Combine all the ingredients, except for the cinnamon sticks, in a large bowl. Toss to mix well.
3. Divide and shape the mixture into 12 balls, then wrap each ball around each cinnamon stick and leave a quarter of the length uncovered.
4. Arrange the beef-cinnamon sticks in the preheated air fryer and spritz with cooking spray.
5. Air fry for 13 minutes or until the beef is browned. Flip the sticks halfway through.
6. Serve immediately.

Fish And Seafood Recipes

Cod With Jalapeño

Servings: 4
Cooking Time: 14 Minutes
Ingredients:
- 4 cod fillets, boneless
- 1 jalapeño, minced
- 1 tablespoon avocado oil
- ½ teaspoon minced garlic

Directions:
1. In the shallow bowl, mix minced jalapeño, avocado oil, and minced garlic.
2. Put the cod fillets in the two air fryer drawers in one layer and top with minced jalapeño mixture.
3. Cook the fish at 185ºC for 7 minutes per side.

Salmon With Cauliflower

Servings: 4
Cooking Time: 25 Minutes
Ingredients:
- 455 g salmon fillet, diced
- 100 g cauliflower, shredded
- 1 tablespoon dried coriander
- 1 tablespoon coconut oil, melted
- 1 teaspoon ground turmeric
- 60 ml coconut cream

Directions:
1. Mix salmon with cauliflower, dried cilantro, ground turmeric, coconut cream, and coconut oil.
2. Transfer the salmon mixture into the air fryer and cook the meal at 176ºC for 25 minutes. Stir the meal every 5 minutes to avoid the burning.

Stuffed Mushrooms With Crab

Servings: 4
Cooking Time: 18 Minutes
Ingredients:
- 907g baby bella mushrooms
- cooking spray
- 2 teaspoons tony chachere's salt blend
- ¼ red onion, diced
- 2 celery ribs, diced
- 227g lump crab
- ½ cup seasoned bread crumbs
- 1 large egg
- ½ cup parmesan cheese, shredded
- 1 teaspoon oregano
- 1 teaspoon hot sauce

Directions:
1. Mix all the ingredients except the mushrooms in a bowl.
2. Divide the crab filling into the mushroom caps.
3. Place the caps in the air fryer baskets.
4. Return the air fryer basket 1 to Zone 1, and basket 2 to Zone 2 of the Tefal 2-Basket Air Fryer.
5. Choose the "Air Fry" mode for Zone 1 at 400 degrees F and 18 minutes of cooking time.
6. Select the "MATCH COOK" option to copy the settings for Zone 2.
7. Initiate cooking by pressing the START/PAUSE BUTTON.
8. Serve warm.

Nutrition:
- (Per serving) Calories 399 | Fat 16g |Sodium 537mg | Carbs 28g | Fiber 3g | Sugar 10g | Protein 35g

Honey Sriracha Mahi Mahi

Servings: 4
Cooking Time: 7 Minutes
Ingredients:
- 3 pounds mahi-mahi
- 6 tablespoons honey
- 4 tablespoons sriracha
- Salt, to taste
- Cooking spray

Directions:
1. In a small bowl, mix the sriracha sauce and honey. Mix well.
2. Season the fish with salt and pour the honey mixture over it. Let it sit at room temperature for 20 minutes.
3. Place a crisper plate in each drawer. Put the fish in a single layer in each. Insert the drawers into the unit.
4. Select zone 1, then AIR FRY, then set the temperature to 400 degrees F/ 200 degrees C with a 7-minute timer. To match zone 2 settings to zone 1, choose MATCH. To begin, select START/STOP.
5. Remove the fish from the drawers after the timer has finished.

Nutrition:
- (Per serving) Calories 581 | Fat 22g | Sodium 495mg | Carbs 26g | Fiber 4g | Sugar 26g | Protein 68g

Salmon Patties

Servings: 8
Cooking Time: 18 Minutes

Ingredients:
- 1 lb. fresh Atlantic salmon side
- ¼ cup avocado, mashed
- ¼ cup cilantro, diced
- 1 ½ teaspoons yellow curry powder
- ½ teaspoons sea salt
- ¼ cup, 4 teaspoons tapioca starch
- 2 brown eggs
- ½ cup coconut flakes
- Coconut oil, melted, for brushing
- For the greens:
- 2 teaspoons organic coconut oil, melted
- 6 cups arugula & spinach mix, tightly packed
- Pinch of sea salt

Directions:
1. Remove the fish skin and dice the flesh.
2. Place in a large bowl. Add cilantro, avocado, salt, and curry powder mix gently.
3. Add tapioca starch and mix well again.
4. Make 8 salmon patties out of this mixture, about a half-inch thick.
5. Place them on a baking sheet lined with wax paper and freeze them for 20 minutes|
6. Place ¼ cup tapioca starch and coconut flakes on a flat plate.
7. Dip the patties in the whisked egg, then coat the frozen patties in the starch and flakes.
8. Place half of the patties in each of the crisper plate and spray them with cooking oil
9. Return the crisper plate to the Tefal Dual Zone Air Fryer.
10. Choose the Air Fry mode for Zone 1 and set the temperature to 390 degrees F and the time to 17 minutes|
11. Select the "MATCH" button to copy the settings for Zone 2.
12. Initiate cooking by pressing the START/STOP button.
13. Flip the patties once cooked halfway through, then resume cooking.
14. Sauté arugula with spinach in coconut oil in a pan for 30 seconds.
15. Serve the patties with sautéed greens mixture

Tilapia Sandwiches With Tartar Sauce

Servings: 4
Cooking Time: 17 Minutes

Ingredients:
- 160 g mayonnaise
- 2 tablespoons dried minced onion
- 1 dill pickle spear, finely chopped
- 2 teaspoons pickle juice
- ¼ teaspoon salt
- ⅛ teaspoon freshly ground black pepper
- 40 g plain flour
- 1 egg, lightly beaten
- 200 g panko bread crumbs
- 2 teaspoons lemon pepper
- 4 (170 g) tilapia fillets
- Olive oil spray
- 4 soft sub rolls
- 4 lettuce leaves

Directions:
1. To make the tartar sauce, in a small bowl, whisk the mayonnaise, dried onion, pickle, pickle juice, salt, and pepper until blended. Refrigerate while you make the fish.
2. Scoop the flour onto a plate; set aside.
3. Put the beaten egg in a medium shallow bowl.
4. On another plate, stir together the panko and lemon pepper.
5. Preheat the air fryer to 205ºC.
6. Dredge the tilapia fillets in the flour, in the egg, and press into the panko mixture to coat.
7. Once the unit is preheated, spray the zone 1 basket with olive oil and place a baking paper liner into the basket. Place the prepared fillets on the liner in a single layer. Lightly spray the fillets with olive oil.
8. cook for 8 minutes, remove the basket, carefully flip the fillets, and spray them with more olive oil. Reinsert the basket to resume cooking.
9. When the cooking is complete, the fillets should be golden and crispy and a food thermometer should register 65ºC. Place each cooked fillet in a sub roll, top with a little bit of tartar sauce and lettuce, and serve.

Orange-mustard Glazed Salmon And Cucumber And Salmon Salad

Servings: 4
Cooking Time: 10 Minutes
Ingredients:
- Orange-Mustard Glazed Salmon:
- 1 tablespoon orange marmalade
- ¼ teaspoon grated orange zest plus 1 tablespoon juice
- 2 teaspoons whole-grain mustard
- 2 (230 g) skin-on salmon fillets, 1½ inches thick
- Salt and pepper, to taste
- Vegetable oil spray
- Cucumber and Salmon Salad:
- 455 g salmon fillet
- 1½ tablespoons olive oil, divided
- 1 tablespoon sherry vinegar
- 1 tablespoon capers, rinsed and drained
- 1 seedless cucumber, thinly sliced
- ¼ white onion, thinly sliced
- 2 tablespoons chopped fresh parsley
- Salt and freshly ground black pepper, to taste

Directions:
1. Make the Orange-Mustard Glazed Salmon :
2. Preheat the air fryer to 205°C.
3. Make foil sling for air fryer basket by folding 1 long sheet of aluminum foil so it is 4 inches wide. Lay sheet of foil widthwise across zone 1 basket, pressing foil into and up sides of basket. Fold excess foil as needed so that edges of foil are flush with top of basket. Lightly spray foil and basket with vegetable oil spray.
4. Combine marmalade, orange zest and juice, and mustard in bowl. Pat salmon dry with paper towels and season with salt and pepper. Brush tops and sides of fillets evenly with glaze. Arrange fillets skin side down on sling in prepared zone 1 basket, spaced evenly apart. Air fry salmon until center is still translucent when checked with the tip of a paring knife and registers 50°C , 10 to 14 minutes, using sling to rotate fillets halfway through cooking.
5. Using the sling, carefully remove salmon from air fryer. Slide fish spatula along underside of fillets and transfer to individual serving plates, leaving skin behind. Serve.
6. Make the Cucumber and Salmon Salad :
7. Preheat the air fryer to 205°C.
8. Lightly coat the salmon with ½ tablespoon of the olive oil. Place skin-side down in the zone 2 air fryer basket and air fry for 8 to 10 minutes until the fish is opaque and flakes easily with a fork. Transfer the salmon to a plate and let cool to room temperature. Remove the skin and carefully flake the fish into bite-size chunks.
9. In a small bowl, whisk the remaining 1 tablespoon olive oil and the vinegar until thoroughly combined. Add the flaked fish, capers, cucumber, onion, and parsley. Season to taste with salt and freshly ground black pepper. Toss gently to coat. Serve immediately or cover and refrigerate for up to 4 hours.

Country Prawns

Servings: 4
Cooking Time: 15 To 20 Minutes
Ingredients:
- 455 g large prawns, peeled and deveined, with tails on
- 455 g smoked sausage, cut into thick slices
- 2 corn cobs, quartered
- 1 courgette, cut into bite-sized pieces
- 1 red bell pepper, cut into chunks
- 1 tablespoon Old Bay seasoning
- 2 tablespoons olive oil
- Cooking spray

Directions:
1. Preheat the air fryer to 204°C. Spray the air fryer drawer lightly with cooking spray.
2. In a large bowl, mix the prawns, sausage, corn, courgette, bell pepper, and Old Bay seasoning, and toss to coat with the spices. Add the olive oil and toss again until evenly coated.
3. Spread the mixture in the two air fryer drawers in a single layer.
4. Air fry for 15 to 20 minutes, or until cooked through, shaking the drawers every 5 minutes for even cooking.
5. Serve immediately.

Bacon-wrapped Shrimp

Servings: 8
Cooking Time: 10 Minutes
Ingredients:
- 24 jumbo raw shrimp, deveined with tail on, fresh or thawed from frozen
- 8 slices bacon, cut into thirds
- 1 tablespoon olive oil
- 1 teaspoon paprika
- 1–2 cloves minced garlic
- 1 tablespoon finely chopped fresh parsley

Directions:
1. Combine the olive oil, paprika, garlic, and parsley in a small bowl.
2. If necessary, peel the raw shrimp, leaving the tails on.
3. Add the shrimp to the oil mixture. Toss to coat well.
4. Wrap a piece of bacon around the middle of each shrimp and place seam-side down on a small baking dish.
5. Refrigerate for 30 minutes before cooking.
6. Place a crisper plate in each drawer. Put the shrimp in a single layer in each drawer. Insert the drawers into the unit.
7. Select zone 1, then AIR FRY, then set the temperature to 360 degrees F/ 180 degrees C with a 10-minute timer. To match zone 2 settings to zone 1, choose MATCH. To begin, select START/STOP.
8. Remove the shrimp from the drawers when the cooking time is over.

Nutrition:
- (Per serving) Calories 479 | Fat 15.7g | Sodium 949mg | Carbs 0.6g | Fiber 0.1g | Sugar 0g | Protein 76.1g

Honey Teriyaki Tilapia

Servings: 4
Cooking Time: 10 Minutes
Ingredients:
- 8 tablespoons low-sodium teriyaki sauce
- 3 tablespoons honey
- 2 garlic cloves, minced
- 2 tablespoons extra virgin olive oil
- 3 pieces tilapia (each cut into 2 pieces)

Directions:
1. Combine all the first 4 ingredients to make the marinade.
2. Pour the marinade over the tilapia and let it sit for 20 minutes.
3. Place a crisper plate in each drawer. Place the tilapia in the drawers. Insert the drawers into the unit.
4. Select zone 1, then AIR FRY, then set the temperature to 360 degrees F/ 180 degrees C with a 10-minute timer. To match zone 2 settings to zone 1, choose MATCH. To begin, select START/STOP.
5. Remove the tilapia from the drawers after the timer has finished.

Nutrition:
- (Per serving) Calories 350 | Fat 16.4g | Sodium 706mg | Carbs 19.3g | Fiber 0.1g | Sugar 19g | Protein 29.3g

Tuna With Herbs

Servings: 4
Cooking Time: 17 Minutes
Ingredients:
- 1 tablespoon butter, melted
- 1 medium-sized leek, thinly sliced
- 1 tablespoon chicken stock
- 1 tablespoon dry white wine
- 455 g tuna
- ½ teaspoon red pepper flakes, crushed
- Sea salt and ground black pepper, to taste
- ½ teaspoon dried rosemary
- ½ teaspoon dried basil
- ½ teaspoon dried thyme
- 2 small ripe tomatoes, puréed
- 120 g Parmesan cheese, grated

Directions:
1. Melt ½ tablespoon of butter in a sauté pan over medium-high heat. Now, cook the leek and garlic until tender and aromatic. Add the stock and wine to deglaze the pan.
2. Preheat the air fryer to 190°C.
3. Grease a casserole dish with the remaining ½ tablespoon of melted butter. Place the fish in the casserole dish. Add the seasonings. Top with the sautéed leek mixture. Add the tomato purée. Cook for 10 minutes in the preheated air fryer. Top with grated Parmesan cheese; cook an additional 7 minutes until the crumbs are golden. Bon appétit!

Smoked Salmon

Servings: 4
Cooking Time: 12
Ingredients:
- 2 pounds of salmon fillets, smoked
- 6 ounces cream cheese
- 4 tablespoons mayonnaise
- 2 teaspoons of chives, fresh
- 1 teaspoon of lemon zest
- Salt and freshly ground black pepper, to taste
- 2 tablespoons of butter

Directions:
1. Cut the salmon into very small and uniform bite-size pieces.
2. Mix cream cheese, chives, mayonnaise, black pepper, and lemon zest, in a small mixing bowl.
3. Let it sit aside for further use.
4. Coat the salmon pieces with salt and butter.
5. Divide the bite-size pieces into both zones of the air fryer.
6. Set it on AIRFRY mode at 400 degrees F for 12 minutes.
7. Select MATCH for zone 2 basket.
8. Hit start, so the cooking start.
9. Once the salmon is done, top it with a bowl creamy mixture and serve.
10. Enjoy hot.

Nutrition:
- (Per serving) Calories 557| Fat 15.7 g| Sodium 371mg | Carbs 4.8 g | Fiber 0g | Sugar 1.1g | Protein 48 g

Tuna Steaks

Servings: 2
Cooking Time: 30 Minutes
Ingredients:
- 2 (6 ounce) boneless tuna steaks
- ¼ cup soy sauce
- 2 teaspoons honey
- 1 teaspoon grated ginger
- 1 teaspoon sesame oil
- ½ teaspoon rice vinegar

Directions:
1. Mix rice vinegar, sesame oil, ginger, honey and soy sauce in a bowl.
2. Pour this marinade over the tuna steaks and cover to marinate for 30 minutes.
3. Place the tuna steaks in the air fryer baskets in a single layer.
4. Return the air fryer basket 1 to Zone 1, and basket 2 to Zone 2 of the Tefal 2-Basket Air Fryer.
5. Choose the "Air Fry" mode for Zone 1 and set the temperature to 380 degrees F and 4 minutes of cooking time.
6. Select the "MATCH COOK" option to copy the settings for Zone 2.
7. Initiate cooking by pressing the START/PAUSE BUTTON.
8. Serve warm.

Nutrition:
- (Per serving) Calories 348 | Fat 30g |Sodium 660mg | Carbs 5g | Fiber 0g | Sugar 0g | Protein 14g

Classic Fish Sticks With Tartar Sauce

Servings: 4
Cooking Time: 12 To 15 Minutes
Ingredients:
- 680 g cod fillets, cut into 1-inch strips
- 1 teaspoon salt
- ½ teaspoon freshly ground black pepper
- 2 eggs
- 70 g almond flour
- 20 g grated Parmesan cheese
- Tartar Sauce:
- 120 ml sour cream
- 120 ml mayonnaise
- 3 tablespoons chopped dill pickle
- 2 tablespoons capers, drained and chopped
- ½ teaspoon dried dill
- 1 tablespoon dill pickle liquid (optional)

Directions:
1. Preheat the air fryer to 204°C. 2. Season the cod with the salt and black pepper; set aside. 3. In a shallow bowl, lightly beat the eggs. In a second shallow bowl, combine the almond flour and Parmesan cheese. Stir until thoroughly combined. 4. Working with a few pieces at a time, dip the fish into the egg mixture followed by the flour mixture. Press lightly to ensure an even coating. 5. Arrange the fish in a single layer in the two air fryer drawers and spray lightly with olive oil. Pausing halfway through the cooking time to turn the fish, air fry for 12 to 15 minutes, until the fish flakes easily with a fork. Let sit in the drawer for a few minutes before serving with the tartar sauce. 6. To make the tartar sauce: In a small bowl, combine the sour cream, mayonnaise, pickle, capers, and dill. If you prefer a thinner sauce, stir in the pickle liquid.

Salmon With Fennel Salad

Servings: 4
Cooking Time: 17 Minutes
Ingredients:
- 2 teaspoons fresh parsley, chopped
- 1 teaspoon fresh thyme, chopped
- 1 teaspoon salt
- 4 (6-oz) skinless center-cut salmon fillets
- 2 tablespoons olive oil
- 4 cups fennel, sliced
- ⅔ cup Greek yogurt
- 1 garlic clove, grated
- 2 tablespoons orange juice
- 1 teaspoon lemon juice
- 2 tablespoons fresh dill, chopped

Directions:
1. Preheat your Tefal Dual Zone Air Fryer to 200 degrees F.
2. Mix ½ teaspoon of salt, thyme, and parsley in a small bowl.
3. Brush the salmon with oil first, then rub liberally rub the herb mixture.
4. Place 2 salmon fillets in each of the crisper plate.
5. Return the crisper plate to the Tefal Dual Zone Air Fryer.
6. Choose the Air Fry mode for Zone 1 and set the temperature to 390 degrees F and the time to 17 minutes|
7. Select the "MATCH" button to copy the settings for Zone 2.
8. Initiate cooking by pressing the START/STOP button.
9. Meanwhile, mix fennel with garlic, yogurt, lemon juice, orange juice, remaining salt, and dill in a mixing bowl.
10. Serve the air fried salmon fillets with fennel salad.
11. Enjoy.

Crumb-topped Sole

Servings: 4
Cooking Time: 7 Minutes
Ingredients:
- 3 tablespoons mayonnaise
- 3 tablespoons Parmesan cheese, grated
- 2 teaspoons mustard seeds
- ¼ teaspoon black pepper
- 4 (170g) sole fillets
- 1 cup soft bread crumbs
- 1 green onion, chopped
- ½ teaspoon ground mustard
- 2 teaspoons butter, melted
- Cooking spray

Directions:
1. Mix mayonnaise with black pepper, mustard seeds, and 2 tablespoons cheese in a bowl.
2. Place 2 sole fillets in each air fryer basket and top them with mayo mixture.
3. Mix breadcrumbs with rest of the ingredients in a bowl.
4. Drizzle this mixture over the sole fillets.
5. Return the air fryer basket 1 to Zone 1, and basket 2 to Zone 2 of the Tefal 2-Basket Air Fryer.
6. Choose the "Air Fry" mode for Zone 1 and set the temperature to 375 degrees F and 7 minutes of cooking time.
7. Select the "MATCH COOK" option to copy the settings for Zone 2.
8. Initiate cooking by pressing the START/PAUSE BUTTON.
9. Serve warm.

Nutrition:
- (Per serving) Calories 308 | Fat 24g |Sodium 715mg | Carbs 0.8g | Fiber 0.1g | Sugar 0.1g | Protein 21.9g

Frozen Breaded Fish Fillet

Servings: 2
Cooking Time: 12
Ingredients:
- 4 Frozen Breaded Fish Fillet
- Oil spray, for greasing
- 1 cup mayonnaise

Directions:
1. Take the frozen fish fillets out of the bag and place them in both baskets of the air fryer.
2. Lightly grease it with oil spray.
3. Set the Zone 1 basket to 380 degrees F fo12 minutes.
4. Select the MATCH button for the zone 2 basket.
5. hit the start button to start cooking.
6. Once the cooking is done, serve the fish hot with mayonnaise.

Nutrition:
- (Per serving) Calories 921| Fat 61.5g| Sodium 1575mg | Carbs 69g | Fiber 2g | Sugar 9.5g | Protein 29.1g

Tuna Patties With Spicy Sriracha Sauce Coconut Prawns

Servings: 6
Cooking Time: 10 Minutes
Ingredients:
- Tuna Patties with Spicy Sriracha Sauce:
- 2 (170 g) cans tuna packed in oil, drained
- 3 tablespoons almond flour
- 2 tablespoons mayonnaise
- 1 teaspoon dried dill
- ½ teaspoon onion powder
- Pinch of salt and pepper
- Spicy Sriracha Sauce:
- 60 g mayonnaise
- 1 tablespoon Sriracha sauce
- 1 teaspoon garlic powder
- Coconut Prawns:
- 230 g medium prawns, peeled and deveined
- 2 tablespoons salted butter, melted
- ½ teaspoon Old Bay seasoning
- 25 g desiccated, unsweetened coconut

Directions:
1. Make the Tuna Patties with Spicy Sriracha Sauce :
2. 1. Preheat the air fryer to 192°C. Line the zone 1 drawer with baking paper. In a large bowl, combine the tuna, almond flour, mayonnaise, dill, and onion powder. Season to taste with salt and freshly ground black pepper. Use a fork to stir, mashing with the back of the fork as necessary, until thoroughly combined. 3. Use an ice cream scoop to form the tuna mixture patties. Place the patties in a single layer on the baking paper in the zone 1 air fryer drawer. Press lightly with the bottom of the scoop to flatten into a circle about ½ inch thick. Pausing halfway through the cooking time to turn the patties, air fry for 10 minutes until lightly browned. 4. To make the Sriracha sauce: In a small bowl, combine the mayonnaise, Sriracha, and garlic powder. Serve the tuna patties topped with the Sriracha sauce.
3. Make the Coconut Prawns :
4. In a large bowl, toss the prawns in butter and Old Bay seasoning.
5. Place shredded coconut in bowl. Coat each piece of prawns in the coconut and place into the zone 2 air fryer drawer.
6. Adjust the temperature to 204°C and air fry for 6 minutes.
7. Gently turn the prawns halfway through the cooking time. Serve immediately.

Roasted Salmon And Parmesan Asparagus

Servings: 4
Cooking Time: 27 Minutes
Ingredients:
- 2 tablespoons Montreal steak seasoning
- 3 tablespoons brown sugar
- 3 uncooked salmon fillets (6 ounces each)
- 2 tablespoons canola oil, divided
- 1-pound asparagus, ends trimmed
- Kosher salt, as desired
- Ground black pepper, as desired
- ¼ cup shredded parmesan cheese, divided

Directions:
1. Combine the steak spice and brown sugar in a small bowl.
2. Brush 1 tablespoon of oil over the salmon fillets, then thoroughly coat with the sugar mixture.
3. Toss the asparagus with the remaining 1 tablespoon of oil, salt, and pepper in a mixing bowl.
4. Place a crisper plate in both drawers. Put the fillets skin-side down in the zone 1 drawer, then place the drawer in the unit. Insert the zone 2 drawer into the device after placing the asparagus in it.
5. Select zone 1, then ROAST, then set the temperature to 390 degrees F/ 200 degrees C with a 17-minute timer. To match the zone 2 settings to zone 1, choose MATCH. To begin cooking, press the START/STOP button.
6. When the zone 2 timer reaches 7 minutes, press START/STOP. Remove the zone 2 drawer from the unit. Flip the asparagus with silicone-tipped tongs. Re-insert the drawer into the unit. Continue cooking by pressing START/STOP.
7. When the zone 2 timer has reached 14 minutes, press START/STOP. Remove the zone 2 drawer from the unit. Sprinkle half the parmesan cheese over the asparagus, and mix lightly. Re-insert the drawer into the unit. Continue cooking by pressing START/STOP.
8. Transfer the fillets and asparagus to a serving plate once they've finished cooking. Serve with the remaining parmesan cheese on top of the asparagus.

Nutrition:
- (Per serving) Calories 293 | Fat 15.8g | Sodium 203mg | Carbs 11.1g | Fiber 2.4g | Sugar 8.7g | Protein 29g

Herb Tuna Patties

Servings: 10
Cooking Time: 12 Minutes
Ingredients:
- 2 eggs
- 425g can tuna, drained & diced
- ½ tsp garlic powder
- ½ small onion, minced
- 1 celery stalk, chopped
- 42g parmesan cheese, grated
- 50g breadcrumbs
- ½ tsp dried oregano
- ½ tsp dried basil
- ½ tsp dried thyme
- 15ml lemon juice
- 1 lemon zest
- Pepper
- Salt

Directions:
1. In a bowl, mix tuna with remaining ingredients until well combined.
2. Insert a crisper plate in the Tefal air fryer baskets.
3. Make patties from the tuna mixture and place them in both baskets.
4. Select zone 1, then select "bake" mode and set the temperature to 380 degrees F for 12 minutes. Press "match" to match zone 2 settings to zone 1. Press "start/stop" to begin. Turn halfway through.

Nutrition:
- (Per serving) Calories 86 | Fat 1.5g |Sodium 90mg | Carbs 4.5g | Fiber 0.4g | Sugar 0.6g | Protein 12.8g

Salmon Nuggets

Servings: 4
Cooking Time: 15 Minutes
Ingredients:
- ⅓ cup maple syrup
- ¼ teaspoon dried chipotle pepper
- 1 pinch sea salt
- 1 ½ cups croutons
- 1 large egg
- 1 (1 pound) skinless salmon fillet, cut into 1 ½-inch chunk
- cooking spray

Directions:
1. Mix chipotle powder, maple syrup, and salt in a saucepan and cook on a simmer for 5 minutes|
2. Crush the croutons in a food processor and transfer to a bowl.
3. Beat egg in another shallow bowl.
4. Season the salmon chunks with sea salt.
5. Dip the salmon in the egg, then coat with breadcrumbs.
6. Divide the coated salmon chunks in the two crisper plates.
7. Return the crisper plate to the Tefal Dual Zone Air Fryer.
8. Select the Air Fry mode for Zone 1 and set the temperature to 390 degrees F and the time to 10 minutes|
9. Press the "MATCH" button to copy the settings for Zone 2.
10. Initiate cooking by pressing the START/STOP button.
11. Flip the chunks once cooked halfway through, then resume cooking.
12. Pour the maple syrup on top and serve warm.

Brown Sugar Garlic Salmon

Servings: 4
Cooking Time: 10 Minutes
Ingredients:
- 455g salmon
- Salt and black pepper, to taste
- 2 tablespoons brown sugar
- 1 teaspoon chili powder
- ½ teaspoon paprika
- 1 teaspoon Italian seasoning
- 1 teaspoon garlic powder

Directions:
1. Mix brown sugar with garlic powder, Italian seasoning, paprika, and chili powder in a bowl.
2. Rub this mixture over the salmon along with black pepper and salt.
3. Place the salmon in the air fryer baskets.
4. Return the air fryer basket 1 to Zone 1, and basket 2 to Zone 2 of the Tefal 2-Basket Air Fryer.
5. Choose the "Air Fry" mode for Zone 1 and set the temperature to 400 degrees F and 10 minutes of cooking time.
6. Select the "MATCH COOK" option to copy the settings for Zone 2.
7. Initiate cooking by pressing the START/PAUSE BUTTON.
8. Flip the salmon once cooked halfway through.
9. Serve warm.

Nutrition:
- (Per serving) Calories 275 | Fat 1.4g |Sodium 582mg | Carbs 31.5g | Fiber 1.1g | Sugar 0.1g | Protein 29.8g

Bacon Halibut Steak

Servings: 4
Cooking Time: 10 Minutes
Ingredients:
- 680 g halibut steaks (170 g each fillet)
- 1 teaspoon avocado oil
- 1 teaspoon ground black pepper
- 110 g bacon, sliced

Directions:
1. Sprinkle the halibut steaks with avocado oil and ground black pepper.
2. Then wrap the fish in the bacon slices and put in the two air fryer baskets.
3. Cook the fish at 200°C for 5 minutes per side.

Pretzel-crusted Catfish

Servings: 4
Cooking Time: 12 Minutes
Ingredients:
- 4 catfish fillets
- ½ teaspoon salt
- ½ teaspoon black pepper
- 2 large eggs
- ⅓ cup Dijon mustard
- 2 tablespoons 2% milk
- ½ cup all-purpose flour
- 4 cups miniature pretzels, crushed
- Cooking spray
- Lemon slices

Directions:
1. Rub the catfish with black pepper and salt.
2. Beat eggs with milk and mustard in a bowl.
3. Spread pretzels and flour in two separate bowls.
4. Coat the catfish with flour then dip in the egg mixture and coat with the pretzels.
5. Place two fish fillets in each air fryer basket.
6. Return the air fryer basket 1 to Zone 1, and basket 2 to Zone 2 of the Tefal 2-Basket Air Fryer.
7. Choose the "Air Fry" mode for Zone 1 at 325 degrees F and 12 minutes of cooking time.
8. Select the "MATCH COOK" option to copy the settings for Zone 2.
9. Initiate cooking by pressing the START/PAUSE BUTTON.
10. Serve warm.

Nutrition:
- (Per serving) Calories 196 | Fat 7.1g | Sodium 492mg | Carbs 21.6g | Fiber 2.9g | Sugar 0.8g | Protein 13.4g

Sole And Cauliflower Fritters And Prawn Bake

Servings: 6
Cooking Time: 24 Minutes
Ingredients:
- Sole and Cauliflower Fritters:
- 230 g sole fillets
- 230 g mashed cauliflower
- 75 g red onion, chopped
- 1 bell pepper, finely chopped
- 1 egg, beaten
- 2 garlic cloves, minced
- 2 tablespoons fresh parsley, chopped
- 1 tablespoon olive oil
- 1 tablespoon coconut aminos or tamari
- ½ teaspoon scotch bonnet pepper, minced
- ½ teaspoon paprika
- Salt and white pepper, to taste
- Cooking spray
- Prawn Bake:
- 400 g prawns, peeled and deveined
- 1 egg, beaten
- 120 ml coconut milk
- 120 g Cheddar cheese, shredded
- ½ teaspoon coconut oil
- 1 teaspoon ground coriander

Directions:
1. Make the Sole and Cauliflower Fritters :
2. 1. Preheat the air fryer to 200°C. Spray the zone 1 air fryer basket with cooking spray. Place the sole fillets in the basket and air fry for 10 minutes, flipping them halfway through. 3. When the fillets are done, transfer them to a large bowl. Mash the fillets into flakes. Add the remaining ingredients and stir to combine. 4. Make the fritters: Scoop out 2 tablespoons of the fish mixture and shape into a patty about ½ inch thick with your hands. Repeat with the remaining fish mixture. 5. Arrange the patties in the zone 1 air fryer basket and bake for 14 minutes, flipping the patties halfway through, or until they are golden brown and cooked through. 6. Cool for 5 minutes and serve on a plate.
3. Make the Prawn Bake :
4. In the mixing bowl, mix prawns with egg, coconut milk, Cheddar cheese, coconut oil, and ground coriander.
5. Then put the mixture in the baking ramekins and put in the zone 2 air fryer basket.
6. Cook the prawns at 205°C for 5 minutes.

Crusted Cod

Servings: 4
Cooking Time: 13 Minutes
Ingredients:
- 2 lbs. cod fillets
- Salt, to taste
- Freshly black pepper, to taste
- ½ cup all-purpose flour
- 1 large egg, beaten
- 2 cups panko bread crumbs
- 1 teaspoon Old Bay seasoning
- Lemon wedges, for serving
- Tartar sauce, for serving

Directions:
1. Rub the fish with salt and black pepper.
2. Add flour in one shallow bowl, beat eggs in another bowl, and mix panko with Old Bay in a shallow bowl.
3. First coat the fish with flour, then dip it in the eggs and finally coat it with the panko mixture.
4. Place half of the seasoned codfish in each crisper plate.
5. Return the crisper plates to the Tefal Dual Zone Air Fryer.
6. Choose the Air Fry mode for Zone 1 and set the temperature to 390 degrees F and the time to 13 minutes
7. Select the "MATCH" button to copy the settings for Zone 2.
8. Initiate cooking by pressing the START/STOP button.
9. Flip the fish once cooked halfway, then resume cooking.
10. Serve warm and fresh with tartar sauce and lemon wedges.

Lemony Prawns And Courgette

Servings: 4
Cooking Time: 7 To 8 Minutes
Ingredients:
- 570 g extra-large raw prawns, peeled and deveined
- 2 medium courgettes (about 230 g each), halved lengthwise and cut into ½-inch-thick slices
- 1½ tablespoons olive oil
- ½ teaspoon garlic salt
- 1½ teaspoons dried oregano
- ⅛ teaspoon crushed red pepper flakes (optional)
- Juice of ½ lemon
- 1 tablespoon chopped fresh mint
- 1 tablespoon chopped fresh dill

Directions:
1. Preheat the air fryer to 176°C.
2. In a large bowl, combine the prawns, courgette, oil, garlic salt, oregano, and pepper flakes and toss to coat.
3. Arrange a single layer of the prawns and courgette in the two air fryer drawers. Air fry for 7 to 8 minutes, shaking the drawer halfway, until the courgette is golden and the prawns are cooked through.
4. Transfer to a serving dish and tent with foil while you air fry the remaining prawns and courgette.
5. Top with the lemon juice, mint, and dill and serve.

Sesame Honey Salmon

Servings: 4
Cooking Time: 10 minutes
Ingredients:
- 4 salmon fillets
- 85g honey
- 15ml sesame oil
- 1 tbsp garlic, minced
- 2 tbsp soy sauce
- 1 tbsp sriracha
- Pepper
- Salt

Directions:
1. In a bowl, coat fish fillets with oil, garlic, honey, sriracha, soy sauce, pepper, and salt. Cover and place in refrigerator for 30 minutes.
2. Insert a crisper plate in the Tefal air fryer baskets.
3. Place the marinated fish fillets in both baskets.
4. Select zone 1, then select "air fry" mode and set the temperature to 375 degrees F for 10 minutes. Press "match" to match zone 2 settings to zone 1. Press "start/stop" to begin.

Nutrition:
- (Per serving) Calories 341 | Fat 14.4g | Sodium 596mg | Carbs 19.5g | Fiber 0.2g | Sugar 17.6g | Protein 35.2g

Foil Packet Salmon

Servings: 4
Cooking Time: 14 Minutes
Ingredients:
- 455g salmon fillets
- 4 cups green beans defrosted
- 4 tablespoons soy sauce
- 2 tablespoons honey
- 2 teaspoons sesame seeds
- 1 teaspoon garlic powder
- ½ teaspoon ginger powder
- ½ teaspoon salt
- ¼ teaspoon white pepper
- ¼ teaspoon red pepper flakes
- Salt, to taste
- Canola oil spray

Directions:
1. Make 4 foil packets and adjust the salmon fillets in each.
2. Divide the green beans in the foil packets and drizzle half of the spices on top.
3. Place one salmon piece on top of each and drizzle the remaining ingredients on top.
4. Pack the salmon with the foil and place two packets in each air fryer basket.
5. Return the air fryer basket 1 to Zone 1, and basket 2 to Zone 2 of the Tefal 2-Basket Air Fryer.
6. Choose the "Air Fry" mode for Zone 1 and set the temperature to 425 degrees F and 14 minutes of cooking time.
7. Select the "MATCH COOK" option to copy the settings for Zone 2.
8. Initiate cooking by pressing the START/PAUSE BUTTON.
9. Serve warm.

Nutrition:
- (Per serving) Calories 305 | Fat 15g | Sodium 482mg | Carbs 17g | Fiber 3g | Sugar 2g | Protein 35g

Cajun Catfish Cakes With Cheese

Servings: 4
Cooking Time: 35 Minutes
Ingredients:
- 2 catfish fillets
- 85 g butter
- 150 g shredded Parmesan cheese
- 150 g shredded Swiss cheese
- 120 ml buttermilk
- 1 teaspoon baking powder
- 1 teaspoon baking soda
- 1 teaspoon Cajun seasoning

Directions:
1. Bring a pot of salted water to a boil. Add the catfish fillets to the boiling water and let them boil for 5 minutes until they become opaque.
2. Remove the fillets from the pot to a mixing bowl and flake them into small pieces with a fork.
3. Add the remaining ingredients to the bowl of fish and stir until well incorporated.
4. Divide the fish mixture into 12 equal portions and shape each portion into a patty.
5. Preheat the air fryer to 190ºC.
6. Arrange the patties in the two air fryer baskets and air fry for 15 minutes until golden brown and cooked through. Flip the patties halfway through the cooking time.
7. Let the patties sit for 5 minutes and serve.

Italian Baked Cod

Servings: 4
Cooking Time: 12 Minutes
Ingredients:
- 4 cod fillets, 170 g each
- 2 tablespoons salted butter, melted
- 1 teaspoon Italian seasoning
- ¼ teaspoon salt
- 120 ml tomato-based pasta sauce

Directions:
1. Place cod into an ungreased round nonstick baking dish. Pour butter over cod and sprinkle with Italian seasoning and salt. Top with pasta sauce.
2. Place dish into the two air fryer drawers. Adjust the temperature to 176ºC and bake for 12 minutes. Fillets will be lightly browned, easily flake, and have an internal temperature of at least 64ºC when done. Serve warm.

Roasted Halibut Steaks With Parsley

Servings: 4
Cooking Time: 10 Minutes
Ingredients:
- 455 g halibut steaks
- 60 ml vegetable oil
- 2½ tablespoons Worcester sauce
- 2 tablespoons honey
- 2 tablespoons vermouth or white wine vinegar
- 1 tablespoon freshly squeezed lemon juice
- 1 tablespoon fresh parsley leaves, coarsely chopped
- Salt and pepper, to taste
- 1 teaspoon dried basil

Directions:
1. Preheat the air fryer to 200°C.
2. Put all the ingredients in a large mixing dish and gently stir until the fish is coated evenly.
3. Transfer the fish to the zone 1 air fryer drawer and roast for 10 minutes, flipping the fish halfway through, or until the fish reaches an internal temperature of at least 64°C on a meat thermometer.
4. Let the fish cool for 5 minutes and serve.

Scallops

Servings: 4
Cooking Time: 5 Minutes
Ingredients:
- ½ cup Italian breadcrumbs
- ½ teaspoon garlic powder
- ¼ teaspoon salt
- ½ teaspoon black pepper
- 2 tablespoons butter, melted
- 1 pound sea scallops, rinsed and pat dry

Directions:
1. Combine the breadcrumbs, garlic powder, salt, and pepper in a small bowl. Pour the melted butter into another shallow bowl.
2. Dredge each scallop in the melted butter, then roll it in the breadcrumb mixture until well covered.
3. Place a crisper plate in each drawer. Put the scallops in a single layer in each drawer. Insert the drawers into the unit.
4. Select zone 1, then AIR FRY, then set the temperature to 360 degrees F/ 180 degrees C with a 5-minute timer. To match zone 2 settings to zone 1, choose MATCH. To begin, select START/STOP.
5. Press START/STOP to pause the unit when the timer reaches 3 minutes. Remove the drawers. Use tongs to carefully flip the scallops over. To resume cooking, re-insert the drawers into the unit and press START/STOP.
6. Remove the scallops from the drawers after the timer has finished.

Nutrition:
- (Per serving) Calories 81 | Fat 6g | Sodium 145mg | Carbs 3g | Fiber 4g | Sugar 1g | Protein 3g

Oyster Po'boy

Servings: 4
Cooking Time: 5 Minutes
Ingredients:
- 105 g plain flour
- 40 g yellow cornmeal
- 1 tablespoon Cajun seasoning
- 1 teaspoon salt
- 2 large eggs, beaten
- 1 teaspoon hot sauce
- 455 g pre-shucked oysters
- 1 (12-inch) French baguette, quartered and sliced horizontally
- Tartar Sauce, as needed
- 150 g shredded lettuce, divided
- 2 tomatoes, cut into slices
- Cooking spray

Directions:
1. In a shallow bowl, whisk the flour, cornmeal, Cajun seasoning, and salt until blended. In a second shallow bowl, whisk together the eggs and hot sauce.
2. One at a time, dip the oysters in the cornmeal mixture, the eggs, and again in the cornmeal, coating thoroughly.
3. Preheat the zone 1 air fryer drawer to 204°C. Line the zone 1 air fryer drawer with baking paper.
4. Place the oysters on the baking paper and spritz with oil.
5. Air fry for 2 minutes. Shake the drawer, spritz the oysters with oil, and air fry for 3 minutes more until lightly browned and crispy.
6. Spread each sandwich half with Tartar Sauce. Assemble the po'boys by layering each sandwich with fried oysters, ½ cup shredded lettuce, and 2 tomato slices.
7. Serve immediately.

Broiled Crab Cakes With Hush Puppies

Servings: 4
Cooking Time: 15 Minutes
Ingredients:
- FOR THE CRAB CAKES
- 2 large eggs
- 2 tablespoons Dijon mustard
- 2 teaspoons Worcestershire sauce
- 1 teaspoon Old Bay seasoning
- ¼ teaspoon paprika
- ¼ cup cracker crumbs (about 9 crackers)
- 1 pound lump crab meat
- 2 teaspoons vegetable oil
- FOR THE HUSH PUPPIES
- ½ cup all-purpose flour
- ⅓ cup yellow cornmeal
- 3 tablespoons sugar
- ¼ teaspoon kosher salt
- ¼ teaspoon baking powder
- 1 large egg
- ½ cup whole milk
- Nonstick cooking spray

Directions:
1. To prep the crab cakes: In a large bowl, whisk together the eggs, mustard, Worcestershire, Old Bay, and paprika until smooth. Stir in the cracker crumbs until fully incorporated, then fold in the crab meat. Refrigerate the crab mixture for 30 minutes.
2. Divide the crab mixture into 8 equal portions. With damp hands, press each portion gently into a loose patty. Brush both sides of each patty with the oil.
3. To prep the hush puppies: In a large bowl, combine the flour, cornmeal, sugar, salt, and baking powder. Stir in the egg and milk to form a stiff batter.
4. Roll the batter into 8 balls. Spritz each hush puppy with cooking spray.
5. To cook the crab cakes and hush puppies: Install a crisper plate in each of the two baskets. Place the crab cakes in a single layer in the Zone 1 basket and insert the basket in the unit. Line the Zone 2 plate with aluminum foil and spray the foil with cooking spray. Arrange the hush puppies on the foil and insert the basket in the unit.
6. Select Zone 1, select AIR BROIL, set the temperature to 400°F, and set the timer to 15 minutes.
7. Select Zone 2, select AIR FRY, set the temperature to 400°F, and set the timer to 7 minutes. Select SMART FINISH.
8. Press START/PAUSE to begin cooking.
9. When cooking is complete, the crab cakes and hush puppies will be golden brown and cooked through. Serve hot.

Nutrition:
- (Per serving) Calories: 403; Total fat: 16g; Saturated fat: 2g; Carbohydrates: 40g; Fiber: 1g; Protein: 27g; Sodium: 872mg

Tuna Patties

Servings: 6
Cooking Time: 10 Minutes
Ingredients:
- For the tuna patties:
- 1 tablespoon extra-virgin olive oil
- 1 tablespoon butter
- ½ cup chopped onion
- ½ red bell pepper, chopped
- 1 teaspoon minced garlic
- 2 (7-ounce) cans or 3 (5-ounce) cans albacore tuna fish in water, drained
- 1 tablespoon lime juice
- 1 celery stalk, chopped
- ¼ cup chopped fresh parsley
- 3 tablespoons grated parmesan cheese
- ½ teaspoon dried oregano
- ¼ teaspoon salt
- Black pepper, to taste
- 1 teaspoon sriracha
- ½ cup panko crumbs
- 2 whisked eggs
- For the crumb coating:
- ½ cup panko crumbs
- ¼ cup parmesan cheese
- Non-stick spray

Directions:
1. In a skillet, heat the oil and butter over medium-high heat.
2. Sauté the onions, red bell pepper, and garlic for 5 to 7 minutes.
3. Drain the tuna from the cans thoroughly. Put the tuna in a large mixing bowl. Add the lime juice.
4. Add the sautéed vegetables to the mixing bowl.
5. Add the celery, parsley, and cheese. Combine well.
6. Add the oregano, salt, and pepper to taste. Mix well.
7. Add a dash of sriracha for a spicy kick and mix well.

8. Add the panko crumbs and mix well.
9. Mix in the eggs until the mixture is well combined. You can add an extra egg if necessary, but the tuna is usually wet enough that it isn't required. Form 6 patties from the mixture.
10. Refrigerate for 30 to 60 minutes (or even overnight).
11. Remove from refrigerator and coat with a mixture of the ½ cup of panko crumbs and ¼ cup of parmesan cheese.
12. Spray the tops of the coated patties with some non-stick cooking spray.
13. Place a crisper place in each drawer. Put 3 patties in each drawer. Insert the drawers into the unit.
14. Select zone 1, then AIR FRY, then set the temperature to 390 degrees F/ 200 degrees C with a 10-minute timer. To match zone 2 settings to zone 1, choose MATCH. To begin, select START/STOP.
15. Remove and garnish with chopped parsley.

Nutrition:
- (Per serving) Calories 381 | Fat 16g | Sodium 1007mg | Carbs 23g | Fiber 2g | Sugar 4g | Protein 38g

Prawns Curry

Servings: 4
Cooking Time: 10 Minutes
Ingredients:
- 180 ml unsweetened full-fat coconut milk
- 10 g finely chopped yellow onion
- 2 teaspoons garam masala
- 1 tablespoon minced fresh ginger
- 1 tablespoon minced garlic
- 1 teaspoon ground turmeric
- 1 teaspoon salt
- ¼ to ½ teaspoon cayenne pepper
- 455 g raw prawns (21 to 25 count), peeled and deveined
- 2 teaspoons chopped fresh coriander

Directions:
1. In a large bowl, stir together the coconut milk, onion, garam masala, ginger, garlic, turmeric, salt and cayenne, until well blended.
2. Add the prawns and toss until coated with sauce on all sides. Marinate at room temperature for 30 minutes.
3. Transfer the prawns and marinade to a baking pan. Place the pan in the zone 1 air fryer drawer. Set the temperature to 192°C for 10 minutes, stirring halfway through the cooking time.
4. Transfer the prawns to a serving bowl or platter. Sprinkle with the cilantro and serve.

Perfect Parmesan Salmon

Servings: 4
Cooking Time:10 Minutes
Ingredients:
- 4 salmon fillets
- 1/4 cup parmesan cheese, shredded
- 1/4 tsp dried dill
- 1/2 tbsp Dijon mustard
- 4 tbsp mayonnaise
- 1 lemon juice
- Pepper
- Salt

Directions:
1. In a small bowl, mix cheese, dill, mustard, mayonnaise, lemon juice, pepper, and salt.
2. Place salmon fillets into the air fryer basket and brush with cheese mixture.
3. Cook salmon fillets at 400 F for 10 minutes.
4. Serve and enjoy.

Shrimp With Lemon And Pepper

Servings: 4
Cooking Time: 8 Minutes
Ingredients:
- 455g raw shrimp, peeled and deveined
- 118ml olive oil
- 2 tablespoons lemon juice
- 1 teaspoon black pepper
- ½ teaspoon salt

Directions:
1. Toss shrimp with black pepper, salt, lemon juice and oil in a bowl.
2. Divide the shrimp into the Tefal 2 Baskets Air Fryer baskets.
3. Return the air fryer basket 1 to Zone 1, and basket 2 to Zone 2 of the Tefal 2-Basket Air Fryer.
4. Choose the "Air Fry" mode for Zone 1 at 350 degrees F and 8 minutes of cooking time.
5. Select the "MATCH COOK" option to copy the settings for Zone 2.
6. Initiate cooking by pressing the START/PAUSE BUTTON.
7. Serve warm.

Nutrition:
- (Per serving) Calories 257 | Fat 10.4g |Sodium 431mg | Carbs 20g | Fiber 0g | Sugar 1.6g | Protein 21g

Breaded Scallops

Servings: 4
Cooking Time: 12 Minutes
Ingredients:
- ½ cup crushed buttery crackers
- ½ teaspoon garlic powder
- ½ teaspoon seafood seasoning
- 2 tablespoons butter, melted
- 1 pound sea scallops patted dry
- cooking spray

Directions:
1. Mix cracker crumbs, garlic powder, and seafood seasoning in a shallow bowl. Spread melted butter in another shallow bowl.
2. Dip each scallop in the melted butter and then roll in the breading to coat well.
3. Grease each Air fryer basket with cooking spray and place half of the scallops in each.
4. Return the crisper plate to the Tefal Dual Zone Air Fryer.
5. Select the Air Fry mode for Zone 1 and set the temperature to 390 degrees F and the time to 12 minutes|
6. Press the "MATCH" button to copy the settings for Zone 2.
7. Initiate cooking by pressing the START/STOP button.
8. Flip the scallops with a spatula after 4 minutes and resume cooking.
9. Serve warm.

Poultry Recipes

Crispy Dill Chicken Strips

Servings: 4
Cooking Time: 10 Minutes
Ingredients:
- 2 whole boneless, skinless chicken breasts (about 450 g each), halved lengthwise
- 230 ml Italian dressing
- 110 g finely crushed crisps
- 1 tablespoon dried dill weed
- 1 tablespoon garlic powder
- 1 large egg, beaten
- 1 to 2 tablespoons oil

Directions:
1. In a large resealable bag, combine the chicken and Italian dressing. Seal the bag and refrigerate to marinate at least 1 hour.
2. In a shallow dish, stir together the potato chips, dill, and garlic powder. Place the beaten egg in a second shallow dish.
3. Remove the chicken from the marinade. Roll the chicken pieces in the egg and the crisp mixture, coating thoroughly.
4. Preheat the air fryer to 170°C. Line the two air fryer drawers with parchment paper.
5. Place the coated chicken on the parchment and spritz with oil.
6. Cook for 5 minutes. Flip the chicken, spritz it with oil, and cook for 5 minutes more until the outsides are crispy and the insides are no longer pink.

Garlic Dill Wings

Servings: 4
Cooking Time: 25 Minutes
Ingredients:
- 900 g bone-in chicken wings, separated at joints
- ½ teaspoon salt
- ½ teaspoon ground black pepper
- ½ teaspoon onion powder
- ½ teaspoon garlic powder
- 1 teaspoon dried dill

Directions:
1. In a large bowl, toss wings with salt, pepper, onion powder, garlic powder, and dill until evenly coated. Place wings into the two ungreased air fryer drawers in a single layer.
2. Adjust the temperature to 200°C and air fry for 25 minutes, shaking the drawer every 7 minutes during cooking. Wings should have an internal temperature of at least 76°C and be golden brown when done. Serve warm.

Chicken Potatoes

Servings: 4
Cooking Time: 22 Minutes
Ingredients:
- 15 ounces canned potatoes drained
- 1 teaspoon olive oil
- 1 teaspoon Lawry's seasoned salt
- ⅛ teaspoons black pepper optional
- 8 ounces boneless chicken breast cubed
- ¼ teaspoon paprika
- ⅜ cup cheddar, shredded
- 4 bacon slices, cooked, cut into strips

Directions:
1. Dice the chicken into small pieces and toss them with olive oil and spices.
2. Drain and dice the potato pieces into smaller cubes.
3. Add potato to the chicken and mix well to coat.
4. Spread the mixture in the two crisper plates in a single layer.
5. Return the crisper plates to the Tefal Dual Zone Air Fryer.
6. Choose the Air Fry mode for Zone 1 and set the temperature to 390 degrees F and the time to 22 minutes|
7. Select the "MATCH" button to copy the settings for Zone 2.
8. Initiate cooking by pressing the START/STOP button.
9. Top the chicken and potatoes with cheese and bacon.
10. Return the crisper plates to the Tefal Dual Zone Air Fryer.
11. Select the Max Crisp mode for Zone 1 and set the temperature to 300 degrees F and the time to 5 minutes|
12. Initiate cooking by pressing the START/STOP button.
13. Repeat the same step for Zone 2 to broil the potatoes and chicken in the right drawer.
14. Enjoy with dried herbs on top.

Chicken Parmesan

Servings: 4
Cooking Time: 10 Minutes
Ingredients:
- Oil, for spraying
- 2 (230 g) boneless, skinless chicken breasts
- 120 g Italian-style bread crumbs
- 20 g grated Parmesan cheese, plus 45 g shredded
- 4 tablespoons unsalted butter, melted
- 115 g marinara sauce

Directions:
1. Preheat the air fryer to 180°C. Line the two air fryer drawers with parchment and spray lightly with oil.
2. Cut each chicken breast in half through its thickness to make 4 thin cutlets. Using a meat tenderizer, pound each cutlet until it is about ¾ inch thick.
3. On a plate, mix together the bread crumbs and grated Parmesan cheese.
4. Lightly brush the chicken with the melted butter, then dip into the bread crumb mixture.
5. Place the chicken in the two prepared drawers and spray lightly with oil.
6. Cook for 6 minutes. Top the chicken with the marinara and shredded Parmesan cheese, dividing evenly. Cook for another 3 to 4 minutes, or until golden brown, crispy, and the internal temperature reaches 76°C.

Lemon Thyme Roasted Chicken

Servings: 6
Cooking Time: 60 Minutes
Ingredients:
- 2 tablespoons baking powder
- 1 teaspoon smoked paprika
- Sea salt and freshly ground black pepper, to taste
- 900 g chicken wings or chicken drumettes
- Avocado oil spray
- 80 ml avocado oil
- 120 ml Buffalo hot sauce, such as Frank's RedHot
- 4 tablespoons unsalted butter
- 2 tablespoons apple cider vinegar
- 1 teaspoon minced garlic

Directions:
1. In a large bowl, stir together the baking powder, smoked paprika, and salt and pepper to taste. Add the chicken wings and toss to coat.
2. Set the air fryer to 200°C. Spray the wings with oil.
3. Place the wings in the two drawers in a single layer and air fry for 20 to 25 minutes. Check with an instant-read thermometer and remove when they reach 70°C. Let rest until they reach 76°C.
4. While the wings are cooking, whisk together the avocado oil, hot sauce, butter, vinegar, and garlic in a small saucepan over medium-low heat until warm.
5. When the wings are done cooking, toss them with the Buffalo sauce. Serve warm.

Coriander Lime Chicken Thighs

Servings: 4
Cooking Time: 22 Minutes
Ingredients:
- 4 bone-in, skin-on chicken thighs
- 1 teaspoon baking powder
- ½ teaspoon garlic powder
- 2 teaspoons chili powder
- 1 teaspoon cumin
- 2 medium limes
- 5 g chopped fresh coriander

Directions:
1. Pat chicken thighs dry and sprinkle with baking powder.
2. In a small bowl, mix garlic powder, chili powder, and cumin and sprinkle evenly over thighs, gently rubbing on and under chicken skin.
3. Cut one lime in half and squeeze juice over thighs. Place chicken into the zone 1 air fryer drawer.
4. Adjust the temperature to 190°C and roast for 22 minutes.
5. Cut other lime into four wedges for serving and garnish cooked chicken with wedges and coriander.

Buffalo Chicken

Servings: 4
Cooking Time: 22 Minutes
Ingredients:
- ½ cup plain fat-free Greek yogurt
- ¼ cup egg substitute
- 1 tablespoon plus 1 teaspoon hot sauce
- 1 cup panko breadcrumbs
- 1 tablespoon sweet paprika
- 1 tablespoon garlic pepper seasoning
- 1 tablespoon cayenne pepper
- 1-pound skinless, boneless chicken breasts, cut into 1-inch strips

Directions:
1. Combine the Greek yogurt, egg substitute, and hot sauce in a mixing bowl.
2. In a separate bowl, combine the panko breadcrumbs, paprika, garlic powder, and cayenne pepper.
3. Dip the chicken strips in the yogurt mixture, then coat them in the breadcrumb mixture.
4. Install a crisper plate in both drawers. Place the chicken strips into the drawers and then insert the drawers into the unit.
5. Select zone 1, select AIR FRY, set temperature to 390 degrees F/ 200 degrees C, and set time to 22 minutes. Select MATCH to match zone 2 settings to zone 1. Press the START/STOP button to begin cooking.
6. When cooking is complete, serve immediately.

Nutrition:
- (Per serving) Calories 234 | Fat 15.8g | Sodium 696mg | Carbs 22.1g | Fiber 1.1g | Sugar 1.7g | Protein 31.2g

Balsamic Duck Breast

Servings: 2
Cooking Time: 20 Minutes
Ingredients:
- 2 duck breasts
- 1 teaspoon parsley
- Salt and black pepper, to taste
- Marinade:
- 1 tablespoon olive oil
- ½ teaspoon French mustard
- 1 teaspoon dried garlic
- 2 teaspoons honey
- ½ teaspoon balsamic vinegar

Directions:
1. Mix olive oil, mustard, garlic, honey, and balsamic vinegar in a bowl.
2. Add duck breasts to the marinade and rub well.
3. Place one duck breast in each crisper plate.
4. Return the crisper plates to the Tefal Dual Zone Air Fryer.
5. Choose the Air Fry mode for Zone 1 and set the temperature to 360 degrees F and the time to 20 minutes|
6. Select the "MATCH" button to copy the settings for Zone 2.
7. Initiate cooking by pressing the START/STOP button.
8. Flip the duck breasts once cooked halfway through, then resume cooking.
9. Serve warm.

General Tso's Chicken

Servings: 4
Cooking Time: 22 Minutes
Ingredients:
- 1 egg, large
- ⅓ cup 2 teaspoons cornstarch,
- ¼ teaspoons salt
- ¼ teaspoons ground white pepper
- 7 tablespoons chicken broth
- 2 tablespoons soy sauce
- 2 tablespoons ketchup
- 2 teaspoons sugar
- 2 teaspoons unseasoned rice vinegar
- 1 ½ tablespoons canola oil
- 4 chile de árbol, chopped and seeds discarded
- 1 tablespoon chopped fresh ginger
- 1 tablespoon garlic, chopped
- 2 tablespoons green onion, sliced
- 1 teaspoon toasted sesame oil
- 1 lb. boneless chicken thighs, cut into 1 ¼ -inch chunks
- ½ teaspoon toasted sesame seeds

Directions:
1. Add egg to a large bowl and beat it with a fork.
2. Add chicken to the egg and coat it well.
3. Whisk ⅓ cup of cornstarch with black pepper and salt in a small bowl.
4. Add chicken to the cornstarch mixture and mix well to coat.
5. Divide the chicken in the two crisper plates and spray them cooking oi.
6. Return the crisper plates to the Tefal Dual Zone Air Fryer.
7. Choose the Air Fry mode for Zone 1 and set the temperature to 390 degrees F and the time to 20 minutes|
8. Select the "MATCH" button to copy the settings for Zone 2.
9. Initiate cooking by pressing the START/STOP button.
10. Once done, remove the air fried chicken from the air fryer.
11. Whisk 2 teaspoons of cornstarch with soy sauce, broth, sugar, ketchup, and rice vinegar in a small bowl.
12. Add chilies and canola oil to a skillet and sauté for 1 minute.
13. Add garlic and ginger, then sauté for 30 seconds.
14. Stir in cornstarch sauce and cook until it bubbles and thickens.
15. Toss in cooked chicken and garnish with sesame oil, sesame seeds, and green onion.
16. Enjoy.

Almond Chicken

Servings: 4
Cooking Time: 25 Minutes
Ingredients:
- 2 large eggs
- ½ cup buttermilk
- 2 teaspoons garlic salt
- 1 teaspoon pepper
- 2 cups slivered almonds, finely chopped
- 4 boneless, skinless chicken breast halves (6 ounces each)

Directions:
1. Whisk together the egg, buttermilk, garlic salt, and pepper in a small bowl.
2. In another small bowl, place the almonds.
3. Dip the chicken in the egg mixture, then roll it in the almonds, patting it down to help the coating stick.
4. Install a crisper plate in both drawers. Place half the chicken breasts in the zone 1 drawer and half in zone 2's, then insert the drawers into the unit.
5. Select zone 1, select AIR FRY, set temperature to 390 degrees F/ 200 degrees C, and set time to 22 minutes. Select MATCH to match zone 2 settings to zone 1. Press the START/STOP button to begin cooking.
6. When the time reaches 11 minutes, press START/STOP to pause the unit. Remove the drawers and flip the chicken. Re-insert the drawers into the unit and press START/STOP to resume cooking.
7. When cooking is complete, remove the chicken.

Nutrition:
- (Per serving) Calories 353 | Fat 18g | Sodium 230mg | Carbs 6g | Fiber 2g | Sugar 3g | Protein 41g

Chicken Drumettes

Servings: 5
Cooking Time: 52 Minutes
Ingredients:
- 10 large chicken drumettes
- Cooking spray
- ¼ cup of rice vinegar
- 3 tablespoons honey
- 2 tablespoons unsalted chicken stock
- 1 tablespoon soy sauce
- 1 tablespoon toasted sesame oil
- ⅜ teaspoons crushed red pepper
- 1 garlic clove, chopped
- 2 tablespoons chopped unsalted roasted peanuts
- 1 tablespoon chopped fresh chives

Directions:
1. Spread the chicken in the two crisper plates in an even layer and spray cooking spray on top.
2. Return the crisper plate to the Tefal Dual Zone Air Fryer.
3. Choose the Air Fry mode for Zone 1 and set the temperature to 390 degrees F and the time to 47 minutes|
4. Select the "MATCH" button to copy the settings for Zone 2.
5. Initiate cooking by pressing the START/STOP button.
6. Flip the chicken drumettes once cooked halfway through, then resume cooking.
7. During this time, mix soy sauce, honey, stock, vinegar, garlic, and crushed red pepper in a suitable saucepan and place it over medium-high heat to cook on a simmer.
8. Cook this sauce for 6 minutes with occasional stirring, then pour it into a medium-sized bowl.
9. Add air fried drumettes and toss well to coat with the honey sauce.
10. Garnish with chives and peanuts.
11. Serve warm and fresh.

Cheddar-stuffed Chicken

Servings: 4
Cooking Time: 20 Minutes
Ingredients:
- 3 bacon strips, cooked and crumbled
- 2 ounces Cheddar cheese, cubed
- ¼ cup barbeque sauce
- 2 (4 ounces) boneless chicken breasts
- Salt and black pepper to taste

Directions:
1. Make a 1-inch deep pouch in each chicken breast.
2. Mix cheddar cubes with half of the BBQ sauce, salt, black pepper, and bacon.
3. Divide this filling in the chicken breasts and secure the edges with a toothpick.
4. Brush the remaining BBQ sauce over the chicken breasts.
5. Place the chicken in the crisper plate and spray them with cooking oil.
6. Return the crisper plate to the Tefal Dual Zone Air Fryer.
7. Choose the Air Fry mode for Zone 1 and set the temperature to 360 degrees F and the time to 20 minutes|
8. Initiate cooking by pressing the START/STOP button.
9. Serve warm.

Wings With Corn On Cob

Servings:2
Cooking Time:40
Ingredients:
- 6 chicken wings, skinless
- 2 tablespoons of coconut amino
- 2 tablespoons of brown sugar
- 1 teaspoon of ginger, paste
- ½ inch garlic, minced
- Salt and black pepper to taste
- 2 corn on cobs, small
- Oil spray, for greasing

Directions:
1. Spay the corns with oil spray and season them with salt.
2. Rub the ingredients well.
3. Coat the chicken wings with coconut amino, brown sugar, ginger, garlic, salt, and black pepper.
4. Spray the wings with a good amount of oil spray.
5. Now put the chicken wings in the zone 1 basket.
6. Put the corn into the zone 2 basket.
7. Select ROAST function for chicken wings, press 1, and set time to 23 minutes at 400 degrees F.
8. Press 2 and select the AIR FRY function for corn and set the timer to 40 at 300 degrees F.
9. Once it's done, serve and enjoy.

Nutrition:
- (Per serving) Calories 950| Fat33.4g | Sodium592 mg | Carbs27. 4g | Fiber2.1g | Sugar11.3 g | Protein129 g

Turkey Meatloaf With Veggie Medley

Servings: 4
Cooking Time: 30 Minutes
Ingredients:
- FOR THE MEATLOAF
- 1 large egg
- ¼ cup ketchup
- 2 teaspoons Worcestershire sauce
- ½ cup Italian-style bread crumbs
- 1 teaspoon kosher salt
- 1 pound ground turkey (93 percent lean)
- 1 tablespoon vegetable oil
- FOR THE VEGGIE MEDLEY
- 2 carrots, thinly sliced
- 8 ounces green beans, trimmed (about 2 cups)
- 2 cups broccoli florets
- 1 red bell pepper, sliced into strips
- 2 tablespoons vegetable oil
- ½ teaspoon kosher salt
- ½ teaspoon freshly ground black pepper

Directions:
1. To prep the meatloaf:
2. In a large bowl, whisk the egg. Stir in the ketchup, Worcestershire sauce, bread crumbs, and salt. Let sit for 5 minutes to allow the bread crumbs to absorb some moisture.
3. Gently mix in the turkey until just incorporated. Form the mixture into a loaf. Brush with the oil.
4. To prep the veggie medley: In a large bowl, combine the carrots, green beans, broccoli, bell pepper, oil, salt, and black pepper. Mix well to coat the vegetables with the oil.
5. To cook the meatloaf and veggie medley:
6. Install a crisper plate in each of the two baskets. Place the meatloaf in the Zone 1 basket and insert the basket in the unit. Place the vegetables in the Zone 2 basket and insert the basket in the unit.
7. Select Zone 1, select ROAST, set the temperature to 350°F, and set the time to 30 minutes.
8. Select Zone 2, select AIR FRY, set the temperature to 390°F, and set the time to 20 minutes. Select SMART FINISH.
9. Press START/PAUSE to begin cooking.
10. When cooking is complete, the meatloaf will be cooked through and the vegetables will be tender and roasted.

Bell Pepper Stuffed Chicken Roll-ups

Servings: 4
Cooking Time: 12 Minutes
Ingredients:
- 2 (115 g) boneless, skinless chicken breasts, slice in half horizontally
- 1 tablespoon olive oil
- Juice of ½ lime
- 2 tablespoons taco seasoning
- ½ green bell pepper, cut into strips
- ½ red bell pepper, cut into strips
- ¼ onion, sliced

Directions:
1. Preheat the air fryer to 200°C.
2. Unfold the chicken breast slices on a clean work surface. Rub with olive oil, then drizzle with lime juice and sprinkle with taco seasoning.
3. Top the chicken slices with equal amount of bell peppers and onion. Roll them up and secure with toothpicks.
4. Arrange the chicken roll-ups in the preheated air fryer. Air fry for 12 minutes or until the internal temperature of the chicken reaches at least 75°C. Flip the chicken roll-ups halfway through.
5. Remove the chicken from the air fryer. Discard the toothpicks and serve immediately.

Turkey And Cranberry Quesadillas

Servings: 4
Cooking Time: 4 To 8 Minutes
Ingredients:
- 6 low-sodium whole-wheat tortillas
- 75 g shredded low-sodium low-fat Swiss cheese
- 105 g shredded cooked low-sodium turkey breast
- 2 tablespoons cranberry sauce
- 2 tablespoons dried cranberries
- ½ teaspoon dried basil
- Olive oil spray, for spraying the tortillas

Directions:
1. Preheat the air fryer to 200°C.
2. Put 3 tortillas on a work surface.
3. Evenly divide the Swiss cheese, turkey, cranberry sauce, and dried cranberries among the tortillas. Sprinkle with the basil and top with the remaining tortillas.
4. Spray the outsides of the tortillas with olive oil spray.
5. One at a time, air fry the quesadillas in the air fryer for 4 to 8 minutes, or until crisp and the cheese is melted. Cut into quarters and serve.

Harissa-rubbed Chicken

Servings: 4
Cooking Time: 21 Minutes
Ingredients:
- Harissa:
- 120 ml olive oil
- 6 cloves garlic, minced
- 2 tablespoons smoked paprika
- 1 tablespoon ground coriander
- 1 tablespoon ground cumin
- 1 teaspoon ground caraway
- 1 teaspoon kosher salt
- ½ to 1 teaspoon cayenne pepper
- Chickens:
- 120 g yogurt
- 2 small chickens, any giblets removed, split in half lengthwise

Directions:
1. For the harissa: In a medium microwave-safe bowl, combine the oil, garlic, paprika, coriander, cumin, caraway, salt, and cayenne. Microwave on high for 1 minute, stirring halfway through the cooking time. 2. For the chicken: In a small bowl, combine 1 to 2 tablespoons harissa and the yogurt. Whisk until well combined. Place the chicken halves in a resealable plastic bag and pour the marinade over. Seal the bag and massage until all of the pieces are thoroughly coated. Marinate at room temperature for 30 minutes or in the refrigerator for up to 24 hours. 3. Arrange the hen halves in a single layer in the two air fryer drawers. Set the air fryer to 200°C for 20 minutes. Use a meat thermometer to ensure the chickens have reached an internal temperature of 76°C.

Herbed Turkey Breast With Simple Dijon Sauce

Servings: 4
Cooking Time: 30 Minutes
Ingredients:
- 1 teaspoon chopped fresh sage
- 1 teaspoon chopped fresh tarragon
- 1 teaspoon chopped fresh thyme leaves
- 1 teaspoon chopped fresh rosemary leaves
- 1½ teaspoons sea salt
- 1 teaspoon ground black pepper
- 1 (900 g) turkey breast
- 3 tablespoons Dijon mustard
- 3 tablespoons butter, melted
- Cooking spray

Directions:
1. Preheat the air fryer to 200°C. Spritz the two air fryer drawers with cooking spray.
2. Combine the herbs, salt, and black pepper in a small bowl. Stir to mix well. Set aside.
3. Combine the Dijon mustard and butter in a separate bowl. Stir to mix well.
4. Rub the turkey with the herb mixture on a clean work surface, then brush the turkey with Dijon mixture.
5. Arrange the turkey in the two preheated air fryer drawers. Air fry for 30 minutes or until an instant-read thermometer inserted in the thickest part of the turkey breast reaches at least 76°C.
6. Transfer the cooked turkey breast on a large plate and slice to serve.

Chicken And Vegetable Fajitas

Servings: 6
Cooking Time: 23 Minutes
Ingredients:
- Chicken:
- 450 g boneless, skinless chicken thighs, cut crosswise into thirds
- 1 tablespoon vegetable oil
- 4½ teaspoons taco seasoning
- Vegetables:
- 50 g sliced onion
- 150 g sliced bell pepper
- 1 or 2 jalapeños, quartered lengthwise
- 1 tablespoon vegetable oil
- ½ teaspoon kosher salt
- ½ teaspoon ground cumin
- For Serving:
- Tortillas
- Sour cream
- Shredded cheese
- Guacamole
- Salsa

Directions:
1. For the chicken: In a medium bowl, toss together the chicken, vegetable oil, and taco seasoning to coat. 2. For the vegetables: In a separate bowl, toss together the onion, bell pepper, jalapeño, vegetable oil, salt, and cumin to coat. 3. Place the chicken in the air fryer basket. Set the air fryer to (190°C for 10 minutes. Add the vegetables to the basket, toss everything together to blend the seasonings, and set the air fryer for 13 minutes more. Use a meat thermometer to ensure the chicken has reached an internal temperature of 75°C. 4. Transfer the chicken and vegetables to a serving platter. Serve with tortillas and the desired fajita fixings.

Spice-rubbed Chicken Pieces

Servings: 6
Cooking Time: 40
Ingredients:
- 3 pounds chicken, pieces
- 1 teaspoon sweet paprika
- 1 teaspoon mustard powder
- 1 tablespoon brown sugar, dark
- Salt and black pepper, to taste
- 1 teaspoon Chile powder, New Mexico
- 1 teaspoon oregano, dried
- ¼ teaspoon allspice powder, ground

Directions:
1. Take a bowl and mix dark brown sugar, salt, paprika, mustard powder, oregano, Chile powder, black pepper, and all spice powder.
2. Mix well and rub this spice mixture all over the chicken.
3. Divide the chicken between two air fryer baskets.
4. Oil sprays the meat and then adds it to the air fryer.
5. Now press button1 and button 2 and set the time to 40 minutes at 350 degrees F.
6. Now press start and once the cooking cycle completes, press pause for both the zones.
7. Take out the chicken and serve hot.

Nutrition:
- (Per serving) Calories353 | Fat 7.1g| Sodium400 mg | Carbs 2.2g | Fiber0.4 g | Sugar 1.6g | Protein66 g

Bang-bang Chicken

Servings: 2
Cooking Time: 20 Minutes
Ingredients:
- 1 cup mayonnaise
- ½ cup sweet chili sauce
- 2 tablespoons Sriracha sauce
- ⅓ cup flour
- 1 lb. boneless chicken breast, diced
- 1 ½ cups panko bread crumbs
- 2 green onions, chopped

Directions:
1. Mix mayonnaise with Sriracha and sweet chili sauce in a large bowl.
2. Keep ¾ cup of the mixture aside.
3. Add flour, chicken, breadcrumbs, and remaining mayo mixture to a resealable plastic bag.
4. Zip the bag and shake well to coat.
5. Divide the chicken in the two crisper plates in a single layer.
6. Return the crisper plate to the Tefal Dual Zone Air Fryer.
7. Choose the Air Fry mode for Zone 1 and set the temperature to 390 degrees F and the time to 20 minutes|
8. Select the "MATCH" button to copy the settings for Zone 2.
9. Initiate cooking by pressing the START/STOP button.
10. Flip the chicken once cooked halfway through.
11. Top the chicken with reserved mayo sauce.
12. Garnish with green onions and serve warm.

Sweet And Spicy Carrots With Chicken Thighs

Servings: 2
Cooking Time: 35
Ingredients:
- Cooking spray, for greasing
- 2 tablespoons butter, melted
- 1 tablespoon hot honey
- 1 teaspoon orange zest
- 1 teaspoon cardamom
- ½ pound baby carrots
- 1 tablespoon orange juice
- Salt and black pepper, to taste
- ½ pound of carrots, baby carrots
- 8 chicken thighs

Directions:
1. Take a bowl and mix all the glaze ingredients in it.
2. Now, coat the chicken and carrots with the glaze and let it rest for 30 minutes.
3. Now place the chicken thighs into the zone 1 basket.
4. Next put the glazed carrots into the zone 2 basket.
5. Press button 1 for the first basket and set it to ROAST Mode at 350 degrees F for 35 minutes.
6. For the second basket hit 2 and set time to AIRFRY mode at 390 degrees F for 8-10 minutes.
7. Once the cooking cycle completes take out the carrots and chicken and serve it hot.

Nutrition:
- (Per serving) Calories 1312| Fat 55.4g| Sodium 757mg | Carbs 23.3g | Fiber6.7 g | Sugar12 g | Protein171 g

Chicken Legs With Leeks

Servings: 6
Cooking Time: 18 Minutes
Ingredients:
- 2 leeks, sliced
- 2 large-sized tomatoes, chopped
- 3 cloves garlic, minced
- ½ teaspoon dried oregano
- 6 chicken legs, boneless and skinless
- ½ teaspoon smoked cayenne pepper
- 2 tablespoons olive oil
- A freshly ground nutmeg

Directions:
1. In a mixing dish, thoroughly combine all ingredients, minus the leeks. Place in the refrigerator and let it marinate overnight.
2. Lay the leeks onto the bottom of the two air fryer drawers. Top with the chicken legs.
3. Roast chicken legs at 190°C for 18 minutes, turning halfway through. Serve with hoisin sauce.

Chicken And Potatoes

Servings: 2
Cooking Time: 10 Minutes
Ingredients:
- 2 potatoes, diced
- 2 chicken breasts, diced
- 4 cloves garlic crushed
- 2 teaspoons smoked paprika
- ½ teaspoon red chili flakes
- 1 teaspoon fresh thyme
- 1 teaspoon salt
- ¼ teaspoon black pepper
- 2 tablespoons olive oil

Directions:
1. Rub chicken with half of the salt, black pepper, oil, thyme, red chili flakes, paprika and garlic.
2. Mix potatoes with remaining spices, oil and garlic in a bowl.
3. Add chicken to one air fryer basket and potatoes the second basket.
4. Return the air fryer basket 1 to Zone 1, and basket 2 to Zone 2 of the Tefal 2-Basket Air Fryer.
5. Choose the "Air Fry" mode for Zone 1 at 375 degrees F and 10 minutes of cooking time.
6. Select the "MATCH COOK" option to copy the settings for Zone 2.
7. Initiate cooking by pressing the START/PAUSE BUTTON.
8. Flip the chicken and toss potatoes once cooked halfway through.
9. Garnish with chopped parsley.
10. Serve chicken with the potatoes.

Nutrition:
- (Per serving) Calories 374 | Fat 13g |Sodium 552mg | Carbs 25g | Fiber 1.2g | Sugar 1.2g | Protein 37.7g

Bbq Cheddar-stuffed Chicken Breasts

Servings: 2
Cooking Time: 25 Minutes
Ingredients:
- 3 strips cooked bacon, divided
- 2 ounces cheddar cheese, cubed, divided
- ¼ cup BBQ sauce, divided
- 2 (4-ounces) skinless, boneless chicken breasts
- Salt and ground black pepper, to taste

Directions:
1. In a mixing bowl, combine the cooked bacon, cheddar cheese, and 1 tablespoon BBQ sauce.
2. Make a horizontal 1-inch cut at the top of each chicken breast with a long, sharp knife, producing a little interior pouch. Fill each breast with an equal amount of the bacon-cheese mixture. Wrap the remaining bacon strips around each chicken breast. Coat the chicken breasts with the leftover BBQ sauce and lay them in a baking dish.
3. Install a crisper plate in both drawers. Place half the chicken breasts in zone 1 and half in zone 2, then insert the drawers into the unit.
4. Select zone 1, select AIR FRY, set temperature to 390 degrees F/ 200 degrees C, and set time to 22 minutes. Select MATCH to match zone 2 settings to zone 1. Press the START/STOP button to begin cooking.
5. When the time reaches 11 minutes, press START/STOP to pause the unit. Remove the drawers and flip the chicken. Re-insert drawers into the unit and press START/STOP to resume cooking.
6. When cooking is complete, remove the chicken breasts.

Nutrition:
- (Per serving) Calories 379 | Fat 12.8g | Sodium 906mg | Carbs 11.1g | Fiber 0.4g | Sugar 8.3g | Protein 37.7g

Italian Chicken & Potatoes

Servings: 4
Cooking Time: 24 Minutes
Ingredients:
- 450g chicken breast, boneless & diced
- 30ml olive oil
- ½ tsp lemon zest
- 2 tbsp fresh lemon juice
- 450g baby potatoes, quartered
- 1 tbsp Greek seasoning
- Pepper
- Salt

Directions:
1. Toss potatoes with ½ tablespoon Greek seasoning, 1 tablespoon oil, lemon zest, lemon juice, pepper, and salt in a bowl.
2. Insert a crisper plate in the Tefal air fryer baskets.
3. Add potatoes into the zone 1 basket.
4. In a bowl, toss chicken with the remaining oil and seasoning.
5. Add the chicken into the zone 2 basket.
6. Select zone 1, then select "air fry" mode and set the temperature to 390 degrees F for 12 minutes. Press "match" to match zone 2 settings to zone 1. Press "start/stop" to begin.

Nutrition:
- (Per serving) Calories 262 | Fat 10.1g |Sodium 227mg | Carbs 15.5g | Fiber 2.9g | Sugar 0.2g | Protein 27.2g

Yummy Chicken Breasts

Servings: 2
Cooking Time: 25
Ingredients:
- 4 large chicken breasts, 6 ounces each
- 2 tablespoons of oil bay seasoning
- 1 tablespoon Montreal chicken seasoning
- 1 teaspoon of thyme
- 1/2 teaspoon of paprika
- Salt, to taste
- oil spray, for greasing

Directions:
1. Season the chicken breast pieces with the listed seasoning and let them rest for 40 minutes.
2. Grease both sides of the chicken breast pieces with oil spray.
3. Divide the chicken breast piece between both baskets.
4. Set zone 1 to AIRFRY mode at 400 degrees F, for 15 minutes.
5. Select the MATCH button for another basket.
6. Select pause and take out the baskets and flip the chicken breast pieces, after 15 minutes.
7. Select the zones to 400 degrees F for 10 more minutes using the MATCH cook button.
8. Once it's done serve.

Nutrition:
- (Per serving) Calories 711| Fat 27.7g| Sodium 895mg | Carbs 1.6g | Fiber 0.4g | Sugar 0.1g | Protein 106.3g

Broccoli Cheese Chicken

Servings: 4
Cooking Time: 25 Minutes
Ingredients:
- 1 tablespoon avocado oil
- 15 g chopped onion
- 35 g finely chopped broccoli
- 115 g cream cheese, at room temperature
- 60 g Cheddar cheese, shredded
- 1 teaspoon garlic powder
- ½ teaspoon sea salt, plus additional for seasoning, divided
- ¼ freshly ground black pepper, plus additional for seasoning, divided
- 900 g boneless, skinless chicken breasts
- 1 teaspoon smoked paprika

Directions:
1. Heat a medium skillet over medium-high heat and pour in the avocado oil. Add the onion and broccoli and cook, stirring occasionally, for 5 to 8 minutes, until the onion is tender.
2. Transfer to a large bowl and stir in the cream cheese, Cheddar cheese, and garlic powder, and season to taste with salt and pepper.
3. Hold a sharp knife parallel to the chicken breast and cut a long pocket into one side. Stuff the chicken pockets with the broccoli mixture, using toothpicks to secure the pockets around the filling.
4. In a small dish, combine the paprika, ½ teaspoon salt, and ¼ teaspoon pepper. Sprinkle this over the outside of the chicken.
5. Set the air fryer to 200ºC. Place the chicken in a single layer in the two air fryer drawers and cook for 14 to 16 minutes, until an instant-read thermometer reads 70ºC. Place the chicken on a plate and tent a piece of aluminum foil over the chicken. Allow to rest for 5 to 10 minutes before serving.

Orange Chicken With Roasted Snap Peas And Scallions

Servings: 4
Cooking Time: 30 Minutes
Ingredients:
- FOR THE CHICKEN
- ⅓ cup all-purpose flour
- 2 large eggs
- ⅓ cup cornstarch, plus 2 tablespoons
- 1½ pounds boneless, skinless chicken breasts, cut into 1-inch pieces
- Nonstick cooking spray
- 2 tablespoons grated orange zest
- 1 cup freshly squeezed orange juice
- ¼ cup granulated sugar
- 2 tablespoons rice vinegar
- 2 tablespoons soy sauce
- ¼ teaspoon minced fresh ginger
- ¼ teaspoon grated garlic
- FOR THE SNAP PEAS
- 8 ounces snap peas
- 1 tablespoon vegetable oil
- ½ teaspoon minced garlic
- ½ teaspoon grated fresh ginger
- ¼ teaspoon kosher salt
- ¼ teaspoon freshly ground black pepper
- 4 scallions, thinly sliced

Directions:
1. To prep the chicken:
2. Set up a breading station with three small shallow bowls. Place the flour in the first bowl. In the second bowl, beat the eggs. Place ⅓ cup of cornstarch in the third bowl.
3. Bread the chicken pieces in this order: First, dip them into the flour to coat. Then, dip into the beaten egg. Finally, add them to the cornstarch, coating all sides. Mist the breaded chicken with cooking spray.
4. In a small bowl, whisk together the orange zest, orange juice, sugar, vinegar, soy sauce, ginger, garlic, and remaining 2 tablespoons of cornstarch. Set orange sauce aside.
5. To prep the snap peas: In a large bowl, combine the snap peas, oil, garlic, ginger, salt, and black pepper. Toss to coat.
6. To cook the chicken and snap peas: Install a crisper plate in the Zone 1 basket. Add the chicken to the basket and insert the basket in the unit. Place the snap peas in the Zone 2 basket and insert the basket in the unit.
7. Select Zone 1, select AIR FRY, set the temperature to 400°F, and set the time to 30 minutes.
8. Select Zone 2, select ROAST, set the temperature to 375°F, and set the time to 12 minutes. Select SMART FINISH.
9. Press START/PAUSE to begin cooking.
10. When the Zone 1 timer reads 15 minutes, press START/PAUSE. Remove the basket and shake to redistribute the chicken. Reinsert the basket and press START/PAUSE to resume cooking.
11. When the Zone 1 timer reads 5 minutes, press START/PAUSE. Remove the basket and pour the reserved orange sauce over the chicken. Reinsert the basket and press START/PAUSE to resume cooking.
12. When cooking is complete, the chicken and vegetables will be cooked through. Stir the scallions into the snap peas. Serve hot.

Thai Curry Chicken Kabobs

Servings: 4
Cooking Time: 15 Minutes
Ingredients:
- 900g skinless chicken thighs
- 120ml Tamari
- 60ml coconut milk
- 3 tablespoons lime juice
- 3 tablespoons maple syrup
- 2 tablespoons Thai red curry

Directions:
1. Mix red curry paste, honey, lime juice, coconut milk, soy sauce in a bowl.
2. Add this sauce and chicken to a Ziplock bag.
3. Seal the bag and shake it to coat well.
4. Refrigerate the chicken for 2 hours then thread the chicken over wooden skewers.
5. Divide the skewers in the air fryer baskets.
6. Return the air fryer basket 1 to Zone 1, and basket 2 to Zone 2 of the Tefal 2-Basket Air Fryer.
7. Choose the "Air Fry" mode for Zone 1 at 350 degrees F and 15 minutes of cooking time.
8. Select the "MATCH COOK" option to copy the settings for Zone 2.
9. Initiate cooking by pressing the START/PAUSE BUTTON.
10. Flip the skewers once cooked halfway through.
11. Serve warm.

Nutrition:
- (Per serving) Calories 353 | Fat 5g |Sodium 818mg | Carbs 53.2g | Fiber 4.4g | Sugar 8g | Protein 17.3g

Chili Chicken Wings

Servings: 4
Cooking Time: 43 Minutes
Ingredients:
- 8 chicken wings drumettes
- cooking spray
- ⅛ cup low-fat buttermilk
- ¼ cup almond flour
- McCormick Chicken Seasoning to taste
- Thai Chili Marinade
- 1 ½ tablespoons low-sodium soy sauce
- ½ teaspoon ginger, minced
- 1 ½ garlic cloves
- 1 green onion
- ½ teaspoon rice wine vinegar
- ½ tablespoon Sriracha sauce
- ½ tablespoon sesame oil

Directions:
1. Put all the ingredients for the marinade in the blender and blend them for 1 minute.
2. Keep this marinade aside. Pat dry the washed chicken and place it in the Ziploc bag.
3. Add buttermilk, chicken seasoning, and zip the bag.
4. Shake the bag well, then refrigerator for 30 minutes for marination.
5. Remove the chicken drumettes from the marinade, then dredge them through dry flour.
6. Spread the drumettes in the two crisper plate and spray them with cooking oil.
7. Return the crisper plate to the Tefal Dual Zone Air Fryer.
8. Choose the Air Fry mode for Zone 1 and set the temperature to 390 degrees F and the time to 43 minutes|
9. Select the "MATCH" button to copy the settings for Zone 2.
10. Initiate cooking by pressing the START/STOP button.
11. Toss the drumettes once cooked halfway through.
12. Now brush the chicken pieces with Thai chili sauce and then resume cooking.
13. Serve warm.

Air-fried Turkey Breast With Roasted Green Bean Casserole

Servings: 4
Cooking Time: 50 Minutes
Ingredients:
- FOR THE TURKEY BREAST
- 2 teaspoons unsalted butter, at room temperature
- 1 bone-in split turkey breast (3 pounds), thawed if frozen
- 1 teaspoon poultry seasoning
- ½ teaspoon kosher salt
- ⅓ teaspoon freshly ground black pepper
- FOR THE GREEN BEAN CASSEROLE
- 1 (10.5-ounce) can condensed cream of mushroom soup
- ½ cup whole milk
- 1 cup store-bought crispy fried onions, divided
- ¼ teaspoon kosher salt
- ¼ teaspoon freshly ground black pepper
- 1 pound green beans, trimmed
- ¼ cup panko bread crumbs
- Nonstick cooking spray

Directions:
1. To prep the turkey breast: Spread the butter over the skin side of the turkey. Season with the poultry seasoning, salt, and black pepper.
2. To prep the green bean casserole: In a medium bowl, combine the soup, milk, ½ cup of crispy onions, the salt, and black pepper.
3. To cook the turkey and beans:
4. Install a crisper plate in the Zone 1 basket. Place the turkey skin-side up in the basket and insert the basket in the unit. Place the green beans in the Zone 2 basket and insert the basket in the unit.
5. Select Zone 1, select AIR FRY, set the temperature to 360°F, and set the time to 50 minutes.
6. Select Zone 2, select ROAST, set the temperature to 350°F, and set the time to 40 minutes. Select SMART FINISH.
7. Press START/PAUSE to begin cooking.
8. When the Zone 2 timer reads 30 minutes, press START/PAUSE. Remove the basket and stir the soup mixture into the beans. Scatter the panko and remaining ½ cup of crispy onions over the top, then spritz with cooking spray. Reinsert the basket and press START/PAUSE to resume cooking.
9. When cooking is complete, the turkey will be cooked through and the green bean casserole will be bubbling and golden brown on top.
10. Let the turkey and casserole rest for at least 15 minutes before serving.
11. Per serving
12. Calories: 577| Total fat: 22g| Saturated fat: 6.5g| Carbohydrates: 24g| Fiber: 3.5g| Protein: 68g| Sodium: 1,165mg

Chicken Wings With Piri Piri Sauce

Servings: 6
Cooking Time: 30 Minutes
Ingredients:
- 12 chicken wings
- 45 g butter, melted
- 1 teaspoon onion powder
- ½ teaspoon cumin powder
- 1 teaspoon garlic paste
- Sauce:
- 60 g piri piri peppers, stemmed and chopped
- 1 tablespoon pimiento, seeded and minced
- 1 garlic clove, chopped
- 2 tablespoons fresh lemon juice
- ⅓ teaspoon sea salt
- ½ teaspoon tarragon

Directions:
1. Steam the chicken wings using a steamer drawer that is placed over a saucepan with boiling water; reduce the heat.
2. Now, steam the wings for 10 minutes over a moderate heat. Toss the wings with butter, onion powder, cumin powder, and garlic paste.
3. Let the chicken wings cool to room temperature. Then, refrigerate them for 45 to 50 minutes.
4. Roast in the preheated air fryer at 170ºC for 25 to 30 minutes; make sure to flip them halfway through.
5. While the chicken wings are cooking, prepare the sauce by mixing all of the sauce ingredients in a food processor. Toss the wings with prepared Piri Piri Sauce and serve.

Chicken & Veggies

Servings: 4
Cooking Time: 10 Minutes
Ingredients:
- 450g chicken breast, boneless & cut into pieces
- 2 garlic cloves, minced
- 15ml olive oil
- 239g frozen mix vegetables
- 1 tbsp Italian seasoning
- ½ tsp chilli powder
- ½ tsp garlic powder
- Pepper
- Salt

Directions:
1. In a bowl, toss chicken with remaining ingredients until well coated.
2. Insert a crisper plate in the Tefal air fryer baskets.
3. Add chicken and vegetables in both baskets.
4. Select zone 1 then select "air fry" mode and set the temperature to 390 degrees F for 10 minutes. Press "match" to match zone 2 settings to zone 1. Press "start/stop" to begin.

Nutrition:
- (Per serving) Calories 221 | Fat 7.6g |Sodium 126mg | Carbs 10.6g | Fiber 3.3g | Sugar 2.7g | Protein 26.3g

Bruschetta Chicken

Servings: 4
Cooking Time: 20 Minutes
Ingredients:
- Bruschetta Stuffing:
- 1 tomato, diced
- 3 tablespoons balsamic vinegar
- 1 teaspoon Italian seasoning
- 2 tablespoons chopped fresh basil
- 3 garlic cloves, minced
- 2 tablespoons extra-virgin olive oil
- Chicken:
- 4 (115 g) boneless, skinless chicken breasts, cut 4 slits each
- 1 teaspoon Italian seasoning
- Chicken seasoning or rub, to taste
- Cooking spray

Directions:
1. Preheat the air fryer to 190º. Spritz the two air fryer baskets with cooking spray.
2. Combine the ingredients for the bruschetta stuffing in a bowl. Stir to mix well. Set aside.
3. Rub the chicken breasts with Italian seasoning and chicken seasoning on a clean work surface.
4. Arrange the chicken breasts, slits side up, in a single layer in the two air fryer baskets and spritz with cooking spray.
5. Air fry for 7 minutes, then open the air fryer and fill the slits in the chicken with the bruschetta stuffing. Cook for another 3 minutes or until the chicken is well browned.
6. Serve immediately.

Chicken With Bacon And Tomato & Bacon-wrapped Stuffed Chicken Breasts

Servings: 8
Cooking Time: 30 Minutes
Ingredients:
- Chicken with Bacon and Tomato:
- 4 medium-sized skin-on chicken drumsticks
- 1½ teaspoons herbs de Provence
- Salt and pepper, to taste
- 1 tablespoon rice vinegar
- 2 tablespoons olive oil
- 2 garlic cloves, crushed
- 340 g crushed canned tomatoes
- 1 small-size leek, thinly sliced
- 2 slices smoked bacon, chopped
- Bacon-Wrapped Stuffed Chicken Breasts:
- 80 g chopped frozen spinach, thawed and squeezed dry
- 55 g cream cheese, softened
- 20 g grated Parmesan cheese
- 1 jalapeño, seeded and chopped
- ½ teaspoon kosher salt
- 1 teaspoon black pepper
- 2 large boneless, skinless chicken breasts, butterflied and pounded to ½-inch thickness
- 4 teaspoons salt-free Cajun seasoning
- 6 slices bacon

Directions:
1. Make the Chicken with Bacon and Tomato :
2. Sprinkle the chicken drumsticks with herbs de Provence, salt and pepper; then, drizzle them with rice vinegar and olive oil.
3. Place into a baking pan and cook in the zone 1 basket at 180°C for 8 to 10 minutes. Pause the air fryer; stir in the remaining ingredients and continue to cook for 15 minutes longer; make sure to check them periodically. Bon appétit!
4. Make the Bacon-Wrapped Stuffed Chicken Breasts :
5. In a small bowl, combine the spinach, cream cheese, Parmesan cheese, jalapeño, salt, and pepper. Stir until well combined.
6. Place the butterflied chicken breasts on a flat surface. Spread the cream cheese mixture evenly across each piece of chicken. Starting with the narrow end, roll up each chicken breast, ensuring the filling stays inside. Season chicken with the Cajun seasoning, patting it in to ensure it sticks to the meat.
7. Wrap each breast in 3 slices of bacon. Place in the zone 2 air fryer basket. Set the air fryer to 180°C for 30 minutes. Use a meat thermometer to ensure the chicken has reached an internal temperature of 75°C.
8. Let the chicken stand 5 minutes before slicing each rolled-up breast in half to serve.

Chicken Fajitas With Street Corn

Servings: 4
Cooking Time: 20 Minutes
Ingredients:
- FOR THE FAJITAS
- 1½ pounds boneless, skinless chicken breasts, cut into strips
- 2 bell peppers (red, orange, yellow, or a combination), sliced into ½-inch-wide strips
- 1 small red onion, sliced
- 1 tablespoon vegetable oil
- 2 teaspoons chili powder
- 1 teaspoon ground cumin
- 1 teaspoon kosher salt
- ½ teaspoon freshly ground black pepper
- ½ teaspoon paprika
- ¼ cup fresh cilantro, chopped
- Juice of 1 lime
- 8 (6-inch) flour tortillas
- FOR THE CORN
- ¼ cup mayonnaise
- ¼ cup sour cream
- ¼ cup crumbled Cotija or feta cheese
- 2 tablespoons chopped fresh cilantro
- 1 teaspoon minced garlic
- ½ teaspoon chili powder
- 4 ears corn, husked

Directions:
1. To prep the fajitas: In a large bowl, combine the chicken, bell peppers, onion, oil, chili powder, cumin, salt, black pepper, and paprika and toss to coat.
2. To prep the corn: In a shallow dish, combine the mayonnaise, sour cream, cheese, cilantro, garlic, and chili powder. Mix well and set aside.
3. To cook the fajitas and corn: Install a crisper plate in each of the two baskets. Place the fajita filling in the Zone 1 basket and insert the basket in the unit. Place the corn ears in the Zone 2 basket and insert the basket in the unit.
4. Select Zone 1, select AIR FRY, set the temperature to 390°F, and set the time to 20 minutes.

5. Select Zone 2, select AIR BROIL, set the temperature to 450°F, and set the time to 12 minutes. Select SMART FINISH.
6. Press START/PAUSE to begin cooking.
7. When both timers read 6 minutes, press START/PAUSE. Remove the Zone 1 basket, shake to redistribute the fajita filling, and reinsert the basket. Remove the Zone 2 basket and use silicone-tipped tongs to flip the corn. Reinsert the basket and press START/PAUSE to resume cooking.
8. When cooking is complete, the chicken will be fully cooked and the vegetables will be slightly charred.
9. Mix the cilantro and lime juice into the fajita filling. Divide the filling among the tortillas. Roll the corn in the mayonnaise and cheese mixture to coat. Serve hot.

Fajita Chicken Strips & Barbecued Chicken With Creamy Coleslaw

Servings: 6
Cooking Time: 20 Minutes
Ingredients:
- Fajita Chicken Strips:
- 450 g boneless, skinless chicken tenderloins, cut into strips
- 3 bell peppers, any color, cut into chunks
- 1 onion, cut into chunks
- 1 tablespoon olive oil
- 1 tablespoon fajita seasoning mix
- Cooking spray
- Barbecued Chicken with Creamy Coleslaw:
- 270 g shredded coleslaw mix
- Salt and pepper
- 2 (340 g) bone-in split chicken breasts, trimmed
- 1 teaspoon vegetable oil
- 2 tablespoons barbecue sauce, plus extra for serving
- 2 tablespoons mayonnaise
- 2 tablespoons sour cream
- 1 teaspoon distilled white vinegar, plus extra for seasoning
- ¼ teaspoon sugar

Directions:
1. Make the Fajita Chicken Strips :
2. Preheat the air fryer to 190°C.
3. In a large bowl, mix together the chicken, bell peppers, onion, olive oil, and fajita seasoning mix until completely coated.
4. Spray the zone 1 air fryer basket lightly with cooking spray.
5. Place the chicken and vegetables in the zone 1 air fryer basket and lightly spray with cooking spray.
6. Air fry for 7 minutes. Shake the basket and air fry for an additional 5 to 8 minutes, until the chicken is cooked through and the veggies are starting to char.
7. Serve warm.
8. Make the Barbecued Chicken with Creamy Coleslaw :
9. Preheat the air fryer to 180°C.
10. Toss coleslaw mix and ¼ teaspoon salt in a colander set over bowl. Let sit until wilted slightly, about 30 minutes. Rinse, drain, and dry well with a dish towel.
11. Meanwhile, pat chicken dry with paper towels, rub with oil, and season with salt and pepper. Arrange breasts skin-side down in zone 2 air fryer basket, spaced evenly apart, alternating ends. Bake for 10 minutes. Flip breasts and brush skin side with barbecue sauce. Return basket to air fryer and bake until well browned and chicken registers 70°C, 10 to 15 minutes.
12. Transfer chicken to serving platter, tent loosely with aluminum foil, and let rest for 5 minutes. While chicken rests, whisk mayonnaise, sour cream, vinegar, sugar, and pinch pepper together in a large bowl. Stir in coleslaw mix and season with salt, pepper, and additional vinegar to taste. Serve chicken with coleslaw, passing extra barbecue sauce separately.

Chipotle Drumsticks

Servings: 4
Cooking Time: 20 Minutes
Ingredients:
- 1 tablespoon tomato paste
- ½ teaspoon chipotle powder
- ¼ teaspoon apple cider vinegar
- ¼ teaspoon garlic powder
- 8 chicken drumsticks
- ½ teaspoon salt
- ⅛ teaspoon ground black pepper

Directions:
1. In a small bowl, combine tomato paste, chipotle powder, vinegar, and garlic powder.
2. Sprinkle drumsticks with salt and pepper, then place into a large bowl and pour in tomato paste mixture. Toss or stir to evenly coat all drumsticks in mixture.
3. Place drumsticks into two ungreased air fryer baskets. Adjust the temperature to 200°C and air fry for 25 minutes, turning drumsticks halfway through cooking. Drumsticks will be dark red with an internal temperature of at least 75°C when done. Serve warm.

Spicy Chicken Sandwiches With "fried" Pickles

Servings: 4
Cooking Time: 18 Minutes
Ingredients:
- FOR THE CHICKEN SANDWICHES
- 2 tablespoons all-purpose flour
- 2 large eggs
- 2 teaspoons Louisiana-style hot sauce
- 1 cup panko bread crumbs
- 1 teaspoon paprika
- ½ teaspoon garlic powder
- ¼ teaspoon salt
- ¼ teaspoon freshly ground black pepper
- ¼ teaspoon cayenne pepper (optional)
- 4 thin-sliced chicken cutlets (4 ounces each)
- 2 teaspoons vegetable oil
- 4 hamburger rolls
- FOR THE PICKLES
- 1 cup dill pickle chips, drained
- 1 large egg
- ½ cup panko bread crumbs
- Nonstick cooking spray
- ½ cup ranch dressing, for serving (optional)

Directions:
1. To prep the sandwiches:
2. Set up a breading station with three small shallow bowls. Place the flour in the first bowl. In the second bowl, whisk together the eggs and hot sauce. Combine the panko, paprika, garlic powder, salt, black pepper, and cayenne pepper in the third bowl.
3. Bread the chicken cutlets in this order: First, dip them into the flour, coating both sides. Then, dip into the egg mixture. Finally, coat them in the panko mixture, gently pressing the breading into the chicken to help it adhere. Drizzle the cutlets with the oil.
4. To prep the pickles:
5. Pat the pickles dry with a paper towel.
6. In a small shallow bowl, whisk the egg. Add the panko to a second shallow bowl.
7. Dip the pickles in the egg, then the panko. Mist both sides of the pickles with cooking spray.
8. To cook the chicken and pickles:
9. Install a crisper plate in each of the two baskets. Place the chicken in the Zone 1 basket and insert the basket in the unit. Place the pickles in the Zone 2 basket and insert the basket in the unit.
10. Select Zone 1, select AIR FRY, set the temperature to 390°F, and set the time to 18 minutes.
11. Select Zone 2, select AIR FRY, set the temperature to 400°F, and set the time to 15 minutes. Select SMART FINISH.
12. Press START/PAUSE to begin cooking.
13. When both timers read 10 minutes, press START/PAUSE. Remove the Zone 1 basket and use silicone-tipped tongs to flip the chicken. Reinsert the basket. Remove the Zone 2 basket and shake to redistribute the pickles. Reinsert the basket and press START/PAUSE to resume cooking.
14. When cooking is complete, the breading will be crisp and golden brown and the chicken cooked through. Place one chicken cutlet on each hamburger roll. Serve the "fried" pickles on the side with ranch dressing, if desired.

Marinated Chicken Legs

Servings: 6
Cooking Time: 28 Minutes
Ingredients:
- 6 chicken legs
- 15ml olive oil
- 1 tsp ground mustard
- 36g brown sugar
- ¼ tsp cayenne
- 1 tsp smoked paprika
- 1 tsp garlic powder
- 1 tsp onion powder
- Pepper
- Salt

Directions:
1. Add the chicken legs and the remaining ingredients into a zip-lock bag. Seal the bag and place in the refrigerator for 4 hours.
2. Insert a crisper plate in the Tefal air fryer baskets.
3. Place the marinated chicken legs in both baskets.
4. Select zone 1, then select "bake" mode and set the temperature to 390 degrees F for 25-28 minutes. Press "match" to match zone 2 settings to zone 1. Press "start/stop" to begin.

Nutrition:
- (Per serving) Calories 308 | Fat 17.9g | Sodium 128mg | Carbs 5.5g | Fiber 0.3g | Sugar 4.7g | Protein 29.9g

Honey Butter Chicken

Servings: 4
Cooking Time: 15 Minutes
Ingredients:
- 4 chicken breasts, boneless
- 85g honey
- 28g butter, melted
- 2 tsp lemon juice
- 15ml olive oil
- 62g Dijon mustard
- Pepper
- Salt

Directions:
1. In a small bowl, mix butter, oil, lemon juice, honey, mustard, pepper, and salt.
2. Insert a crisper plate in the Tefal air fryer baskets.
3. Brush chicken breasts with butter mixture and place them in both baskets.
4. Select zone 1 then select "bake" mode and set the temperature to 380 degrees F for 15 minutes. Press "match" to match zone 2 settings to zone 1. Press "start/stop" to begin.

Nutrition:
- (Per serving) Calories 434 | Fat 20.7g | Sodium 384mg | Carbs 18.4g | Fiber 0.6g | Sugar 17.6g | Protein 43.1g

Desserts Recipes

Soft Pecan Brownies

Servings: 6
Cooking Time: 20 Minutes
Ingredients:
- ½ cup blanched finely ground almond flour
- ½ cup powdered erythritol
- 2 tablespoons unsweetened cocoa powder
- ½ teaspoon baking powder
- ¼ cup unsalted butter, softened
- 1 large egg
- ¼ cup chopped pecans
- ¼ cup low-carb, sugar-free chocolate chips

Directions:
1. Stir erythritol, almond flour, baking powder and cocoa powder in a large bowl. Add in egg and butter, mix well.
2. Fold in chocolate chips and pecans. Pour mixture into 6"| round baking pan. Put pan into the air fryer basket.
3. Set the temperature to 300°F, then set the timer for 20 minutes.
4. A toothpick inserted in center will come out clean when completely cooked. Let it rest for 20 minutes to fully cool and firm up. Serve immediately.

Stuffed Apples

Servings: 8
Cooking Time: 10 Minutes
Ingredients:
- 8 small firm apples, cored
- 1 cup golden raisins
- 1 cup blanched almonds
- 4 tablespoons sugar
- ¼ teaspoon ground cinnamon

Directions:
1. In a food processor, add raisins, almonds, sugar and cinnamon and pulse until chopped.
2. Carefully stuff each apple with raisin mixture.
3. Line each basket of "Zone 1" and "Zone 2" with parchment paper.
4. Press "Zone 1" and "Zone 2" and then rotate the knob for each zone to select "Air Fry".
5. Set the temperature to 355 degrees F/ 180 degrees C for both zones and then set the time for 5 minutes to preheat.
6. After preheating, arrange 4 apples into the basket of each zone.
7. Slide each basket into Air Fryer and set the time for 10 minutes.
8. After cooking time is completed, remove the apples from Air Fryer.
9. Transfer the apples onto plates and set aside to cool slightly before serving.

Chocolate Muffins

Servings: 12
Cooking Time: 20 Minutes
Ingredients:
- 2 cup all-purpose flour
- 4 tablespoons cocoa powder
- ½ teaspoon baking soda
- 2 teaspoons baking powder
- ½ teaspoon salt
- 1 cup coconut milk
- ½ cup granulated sugar
- 6 tablespoons coconut oil, melted
- 1 teaspoon vanilla extract
- 1 cup dark chocolate chips
- ½ cup pistachios, chopped

Directions:
1. In a bowl, add the flour, cocoa powder, baking powder, baking soda, and salt and mix well.
2. In another bowl, add the coconut milk, sugar, coconut oil and vanilla extract and beat until well combined.
3. Add the flour mixture and mix until just combined.
4. Fold in the chocolate chips and pistachios.
5. Grease 2 silicone muffin tins.
6. Place the mixture into prepared muffin cups about ¾ full.
7. Press "Zone 1" and "Zone 2" and then rotate the knob for each zone to select "Air Fry".
8. Set the temperature to 300 degrees F/ 150 degrees C for both zones and then set the time for 5 minutes to preheat.
9. After preheating, arrange 1 muffin tin into the basket of each zone.
10. Slide each basket into Air Fryer and set the time for 15 minutes.
11. After cooking time is completed, remove the muffin tin from Air Fryer.
12. Place the muffin molds onto a wire rack to cool for about 10 minutes.
13. Carefully invert the muffins onto the wire rack to completely cool before serving.

Mini Peanut Butter Tarts

Servings: 8
Cooking Time: 12 To 15 Minutes
Ingredients:
- 125 g pecans
- 110 g finely ground blanched almond flour
- 2 tablespoons unsalted butter, at room temperature
- 50 g powdered sweetener, plus 2 tablespoons, divided
- 120 g heavy (whipping) cream
- 2 tablespoons mascarpone cheese
- 110 g cream cheese
- 140 g sugar-free peanut butter
- 1 teaspoon pure vanilla extract
- ⅛ teaspoon sea salt
- 85 g organic chocolate chips
- 1 tablespoon coconut oil
- 40 g chopped peanuts or pecans

Directions:
1. Place the pecans in the bowl of a food processor; process until they are finely ground.
2. Transfer the ground pecans to a medium bowl and stir in the almond flour. Add the butter and 2 tablespoons of sweetener and stir until the mixture becomes wet and crumbly.
3. Divide the mixture among 8 silicone muffin cups, pressing the crust firmly with your fingers into the bottom and part way up the sides of each cup.
4. Arrange the muffin cups in the two air fryer drawers. Set the air fryer to 148°C and bake for 12 to 15 minutes, until the crusts begin to brown. Remove the cups from the air fryer and set them aside to cool.
5. In the bowl of a stand mixer, combine the heavy cream and mascarpone cheese. Beat until peaks form. Transfer to a large bowl.
6. In the same stand mixer bowl, combine the cream cheese, peanut butter, remaining 50 g sweetener, vanilla, and salt. Beat at medium-high speed until smooth.
7. Reduce the speed to low and add the heavy cream mixture back a spoonful at a time, beating after each addition.
8. Spoon the peanut butter mixture over the crusts and freeze the tarts for 30 minutes.
9. Place the chocolate chips and coconut oil in the top of a double boiler over high heat. Stir until melted, then remove from the heat.
10. Drizzle the melted chocolate over the peanut butter tarts. Top with the chopped nuts and freeze the tarts for another 15 minutes, until set.
11. Store the peanut butter tarts in an airtight container in the refrigerator for up to 1 week or in the freezer for up to 1 month.

Berry Crumble And Coconut-custard Pie

Servings: 8
Cooking Time: 20 To 23 Minutes
Ingredients:
- Berry Crumble:
- For the Filling:
- 300 g mixed berries
- 2 tablespoons sugar
- 1 tablespoon cornflour
- 1 tablespoon fresh lemon juice
- For the Topping:
- 30 g plain flour
- 20 g rolled oats
- 1 tablespoon granulated sugar
- 2 tablespoons cold unsalted butter, cut into small cubes
- Whipped cream or ice cream (optional)
- Coconut-Custard Pie:
- 240 ml milk
- 50 g granulated sugar, plus 2 tablespoons
- 30 g scone mix
- 1 teaspoon vanilla extract
- 2 eggs
- 2 tablespoons melted butter
- Cooking spray
- 50 g desiccated, sweetened coconut

Directions:
1. Make the Berry Crumble :
2. 1. Preheat the air fryer to 205°C. For the filling: In a round baking pan, gently mix the berries, sugar, cornflour, and lemon juice until thoroughly combined.
3. For the topping: In a small bowl, combine the flour, oats, and sugar. Stir the butter into the flour mixture until the mixture has the consistency of breadcrumbs.
4. Sprinkle the topping over the berries. 5. Put the pan in the zone 1 air fryer basket and air fry for 15 minutes. Let cool for 5 minutes on a wire rack. 6. Serve topped with whipped cream or ice cream, if desired.
3. Make the Coconut-Custard Pie :
4. Place all ingredients except coconut in a medium bowl.
5. Using a hand mixer, beat on high speed for 3 minutes.
6. Let sit for 5 minutes.
7. Preheat the air fryer to 165°C.
8. Spray a baking pan with cooking spray and place pan in the zone 2 air fryer basket.
9. Pour filling into pan and sprinkle coconut over top.
10. Cook pie for 20 to 23 minutes or until center sets.

Quickie Cinnamon Sugar Pork Rinds

Servings: 2
Cooking Time: 5 Minutes
Ingredients:
- 2 ounces pork rinds
- 2 tablespoons unsalted butter, melted
- ½ teaspoon ground cinnamon
- ¼ cup powdered erythritol

Directions:
1. Stir butter and pork rinds in a large bowl. Sprinkle with erythritol and cinnamon, then toss to coat well.
2. Put pork rinds into the air fryer basket.
3. Set the temperature to 400°F, then set the timer for 5 minutes.
4. Serve warm.

Mini Strawberry And Cream Pies

Servings: 2
Cooking Time: 15 Minutes
Ingredients:
- 1 box store-bought pie dough, Trader Joe's
- 1 cup strawberries, cubed
- 3 tablespoons cream, heavy
- 2 tablespoons almonds
- 1 egg white, for brushing

Directions:
1. Take the store-bought pie dough and flatten it on a surface.
2. Use a round cutter to cut it into 3-inch circles.
3. Brush the dough with egg white all around the edges.
4. Now add almonds, strawberries, and cream in a tiny amount in the center of the dough, and top it with another dough circle.
5. Press the edges with a fork to seal it.
6. Make a slit in the middle of the pie and divide them into the baskets.
7. Set zone 1 to AIR FRY mode 360 degrees F for 10 minutes.
8. Select MATCH for zone 2 basket.
9. Once done, serve.

Olive Oil Cake & Old-fashioned Fudge Pie

Servings: 16
Cooking Time: 30 Minutes
Ingredients:
- Olive Oil Cake:
- 120 g blanched finely ground almond flour
- 5 large eggs, whisked
- 175 ml extra-virgin olive oil
- 75 g granulated sweetener
- 1 teaspoon vanilla extract
- 1 teaspoon baking powder
- Old-Fashioned Fudge Pie:
- 300 g granulated sugar
- 40 g unsweetened cocoa powder
- 70 g self-raising flour
- 3 large eggs, unbeaten
- 12 tablespoons unsalted butter, melted
- 1½ teaspoons vanilla extract
- 1 (9-inch) unbaked piecrust
- 30 g icing sugar (optional)

Directions:
1. Make the Olive Oil Cake :
2. In a large bowl, mix all ingredients. Pour batter into an ungreased round nonstick baking dish.
3. Place dish into the zone 1 air fryer basket. Adjust the temperature to 150ºC and bake for 30 minutes. The cake will be golden on top and firm in the center when done.
4. Let cake cool in dish 30 minutes before slicing and serving.
5. Make the Old-Fashioned Fudge Pie :
6. In a medium bowl, stir together the sugar, cocoa powder, and flour. Stir in the eggs and melted butter. Stir in the vanilla.
7. Preheat the air fryer to 175ºC.
8. Pour the chocolate filing into the crust.
9. Cook in the zone 2 basket for 25 to 30 minutes, stirring every 10 minutes, until a knife inserted into the middle comes out clean. Let sit for 5 minutes before dusting with icing sugar to serve.

Lime Bars

Servings: 12 Bars
Cooking Time: 33 Minutes
Ingredients:
- 140 g blanched finely ground almond flour, divided
- 75 g powdered sweetener, divided
- 4 tablespoons salted butter, melted
- 120 ml fresh lime juice
- 2 large eggs, whisked

Directions:
1. In a medium bowl, mix together 110 g flour, 25 g sweetener, and butter. Press mixture into bottom of an ungreased round nonstick cake pan.
2. Place pan into the zone 1 air fryer drawer. Adjust the temperature to 148ºC and bake for 13 minutes. Crust will be brown and set in the middle when done.
3. Allow to cool in pan 10 minutes.
4. In a medium bowl, combine remaining flour, remaining sweetener, lime juice, and eggs. Pour mixture over cooled crust and return to air fryer for 20 minutes. Top will be browned and firm when done.
5. Let cool completely in pan, about 30 minutes, then chill covered in the refrigerator 1 hour. Serve chilled.

Healthy Semolina Pudding

Servings: 4
Cooking Time: 20 Minutes
Ingredients:
- 45g semolina
- 1 tsp vanilla
- 500ml milk
- 115g caster sugar

Directions:
1. Mix semolina and ½ cup milk in a bowl. Slowly add the remaining milk, sugar, and vanilla and mix well.
2. Pour the mixture into four greased ramekins.
3. Insert a crisper plate in the Tefal air fryer baskets.
4. Place ramekins in both baskets.
5. Select zone 1, then select "air fry" mode and set the temperature to 300 degrees F for 20 minutes. Press "match" to match zone 2 settings to zone 1. Press "start/stop" to begin.

Nutrition:
- (Per serving) Calories 209 | Fat 2.7g |Sodium 58mg | Carbs 41.5g | Fiber 0.6g | Sugar 30.6g | Protein 5.8g

Moist Chocolate Espresso Muffins

Servings: 8
Cooking Time: 18 Minutes
Ingredients:
- 1 egg
- 177ml milk
- ½ tsp baking soda
- ½ tsp espresso powder
- ½ tsp baking powder
- 50g cocoa powder
- 78ml vegetable oil
- 1 tsp apple cider vinegar
- 1 tsp vanilla
- 150g brown sugar
- 150g all-purpose flour
- ½ tsp salt

Directions:
1. In a bowl, whisk egg, vinegar, oil, brown sugar, vanilla, and milk.
2. Add flour, cocoa powder, baking soda, baking powder, espresso powder, and salt and stir until well combined.
3. Pour batter into the silicone muffin moulds.
4. Insert a crisper plate in Tefal air fryer baskets.
5. Place muffin moulds in both baskets.
6. Select zone 1 then select "bake" mode and set the temperature to 320 degrees F for 18 minutes. Press match cook to match zone 2 settings to zone 1. Press "start/stop" to begin.

Nutrition:
- (Per serving) Calories 222 | Fat 11g |Sodium 251mg | Carbs 29.6g | Fiber 2g | Sugar 14.5g | Protein 4g

Fluffy Layered Peanut Butter Cheesecake Brownies

Servings: 6
Cooking Time: 35 Minutes
Ingredients:
- ½ cup blanched finely ground almond flour
- 1 cup powdered erythritol, divided
- 2 tablespoons unsweetened cocoa powder
- ½ teaspoon baking powder
- ¼ cup unsalted butter, softened
- 2 large eggs, divided
- 8 ounces full-fat cream cheese, softened
- ¼ cup heavy whipping cream
- 1 teaspoon vanilla extract
- 2 tablespoons no-sugar-added peanut butter

Directions:
1. In a large bowl, combine ½ cup erythritol, almond flour, baking powder and cocoa powder. Add in butter and one egg, stir well.
2. Spoon mixture into 6&quot| round baking pan. Put pan into the air fryer basket.
3. Set the temperature to 300°F, then set the timer for 20 minutes.
4. A toothpick inserted in center will come out clean when fully cooked. Allow to completely cool for 20 minutes and firm up.
5. In a large bowl, beat heavy cream, cream cheese, remaining ½ cup erythritol, peanut butter, remaining egg, and vanilla until turns fluffy.
6. Spoon mixture over cooled brownies. Return the pan into the air fryer basket.
7. Set the temperature to 300°F, then set the timer for 15 minutes.
8. When fully done, cheesecake will be slightly browned and mostly firm with
9. a slight jiggle. Let it rest and refrigerate for at least 2 hours before serving.

Lemony Sweet Twists

Servings: 2
Cooking Time: 10 Minutes
Ingredients:
- 1 box store-bought puff pastry
- ½ teaspoon lemon zest
- 1 tablespoon lemon juice
- 2 teaspoons brown sugar
- Salt, pinch
- 2 tablespoons Parmesan cheese, freshly grated

Directions:
1. Put the puff pastry dough on a clean work surface.
2. In a bowl, combine Parmesan cheese, brown sugar, salt, lemon zest, and lemon juice.
3. Press this mixture into both sides of the dough.
4. Now, cut the pastry into 1" x 4" strips.
5. Twist 2 times from each end.
6. Place the strips into the air fryer baskets.
7. Select zone 1 to AIR FRY mode at 400 degrees F for 9-10 minutes.
8. Select MATCH for zone 2 basket.
9. Once cooked, serve and enjoy.

Fudge Brownies

Servings: 4
Cooking Time: 15 Minutes
Ingredients:
- ½ cup all-purpose flour
- ¼ cup unsweetened cocoa powder
- ¾ teaspoon kosher salt
- 2 large eggs, whisked
- 1 tablespoon almond milk
- ½ cup brown sugar
- ½ cup packed white sugar
- ½ tablespoon vanilla extract
- 8 ounces semisweet chocolate chips, melted
- ½ cup unsalted butter, melted

Directions:
1. Take a medium bowl, and use a hand beater to whisk together eggs, milk, both the sugars and vanilla.
2. In a separate microwave-safe bowl, mix the melted butter and chocolate and microwave it for 30 seconds to melt the chocolate.
3. Add all the dry to the chocolate mixture.
4. Slowly add the egg mixture to the bowl.
5. Spray a reasonable round baking pan and pour the batter into the pan.
6. Select the AIR FRY mode and adjust the setting the temperature to 300 degrees F, for 30 minutes.
7. Check it after 30 minutes and if not done, cook for 10 more minutes.
8. Once it's done, take it out and let it cool before serving.
9. Enjoy.

Cinnamon Bread Twists

Servings: 4
Cooking Time: 15 Minutes
Ingredients:
- Bread Twists Dough
- 120g all-purpose flour
- 1 teaspoon baking powder
- ¼ teaspoon salt
- 150g fat free Greek yogurt
- Brushing
- 2 tablespoons light butter
- 2 tablespoons granulated sugar
- 1-2 teaspoons ground cinnamon, to taste

Directions:
1. Mix flour, salt and baking powder in a bowl.
2. Stir in yogurt and the rest of the dough ingredients in a bowl.
3. Mix well and make 8 inches long strips out of this dough.
4. Twist the strips and place them in the air fryer baskets.
5. Return the air fryer basket 1 to Zone 1, and basket 2 to Zone 2 of the Tefal 2-Basket Air Fryer.
6. Choose the "Air Fry" mode for Zone 1 at 375 degrees F and 15 minutes of cooking time.
7. Select the "MATCH COOK" option to copy the settings for Zone 2.
8. Initiate cooking by pressing the START/PAUSE BUTTON.
9. Flip the twists once cooked halfway through.
10. Mix butter with cinnamon and sugar in a bowl.
11. Brush this mixture over the twists.
12. Serve.

Nutrition:
- (Per serving) Calories 391 | Fat 24g |Sodium 142mg | Carbs 38.5g | Fiber 3.5g | Sugar 21g | Protein 6.6g

Easy Mini Chocolate Chip Pan Cookie

Servings: 4
Cooking Time: 7 Minutes
Ingredients:
- ½ cup blanched finely ground almond flour
- ¼ cup powdered erythritol
- 2 tablespoons unsalted butter, softened
- 1 large egg
- ½ teaspoon unflavored gelatin
- ½ teaspoon baking powder
- ½ teaspoon vanilla extract
- 2 tablespoons low-carb, sugar-free chocolate chips

Directions:
1. Combine erythritol and almond flour in a large bowl. Add in egg, gelatin, and butter , stir well.
2. Stir in vanilla and baking powder and then fold in chocolate chips. Spoon batter into 6&quot| round baking pan. Put pan into the air fryer basket.
3. Set the temperature to 300°F, then set the timer for 7 minutes.
4. The top of the cookie will be golden brown and a toothpick inserted in center will come out clean when fully cooked. Allow to rest for more than 10 minutes.

Apple Nutmeg Flautas

Servings: 8
Cooking Time: 8 Minutes.
Ingredients:
- ¼ cup light brown sugar
- ⅛ cup all-purpose flour
- ¼ teaspoon ground cinnamon
- Nutmeg, to taste
- 4 apples, peeled, cored & sliced
- ½ lemon, juice, and zest
- 6 (10-inch) flour tortillas
- Vegetable oil
- Caramel sauce
- Cinnamon sugar

Directions:
1. Mix brown sugar with cinnamon, nutmeg, and flour in a large bowl.
2. Toss in apples in lemon juice. Mix well.
3. Place a tortilla at a time on a flat surface and add ½ cup of the apple mixture to the tortilla.
4. Roll the tortilla into a burrito and seal it tightly and hold it in place with a toothpick.
5. Repeat the same steps with the remaining tortillas and apple mixture.
6. Place two apple burritos in each of the crisper plate and spray them with cooking oil.
7. Return the crisper plates to the Tefal Dual Zone Air Fryer.
8. Choose the Air Fry mode for Zone 1 and set the temperature to 400 degrees F and the time to 8 minutes.
9. Select the "MATCH" button to copy the settings for Zone 2.
10. Initiate cooking by pressing the START/STOP button.
11. Flip the burritos once cooked halfway through, then resume cooking.
12. Garnish with caramel sauce and cinnamon sugar.
13. Enjoy!

Nutrition:
- (Per serving) Calories 157 | Fat 1.3g |Sodium 27mg | Carbs 1.3g | Fiber 1g | Sugar 2.2g | Protein 8.2g

Walnuts Fritters

Servings: 6
Cooking Time: 15 Minutes.
Ingredients:
- 1 cup all-purpose flour
- ½ cup walnuts, chopped
- ¼ cup white sugar
- ¼ cup milk
- 1 egg
- 1 ½ teaspoons baking powder
- 1 pinch salt
- Cooking spray
- 2 tablespoons white sugar
- ½ teaspoon ground cinnamon
- Glaze:
- ½ cup confectioners' sugar
- 1 tablespoon milk
- ½ teaspoon caramel extract
- ¼ teaspoons ground cinnamon

Directions:
1. Layer both crisper plate with parchment paper.
2. Grease the parchment paper with cooking spray.
3. Whisk flour with milk, ¼ cup of sugar, egg, baking powder, and salt in a small bowl.
4. Separately mix 2 tablespoons of sugar with cinnamon in another bowl, toss in walnuts and mix well to coat.
5. Stir in flour mixture and mix until combined.
6. Drop the fritters mixture using a cookie scoop into the two crisper plate.
7. Return the crisper plate to the Tefal Dual Zone Air Fryer.
8. Choose the Air Fry mode for Zone 1 and set the temperature to 375 degrees F and the time to 15 minutes.
9. Select the "MATCH" button to copy the settings for Zone 2.
10. Initiate cooking by pressing the START/STOP button.
11. Flip the fritters once cooked halfway through, then resume cooking.
12. Meanwhile, whisk milk, caramel extract, confectioners' sugar, and cinnamon in a bowl.
13. Transfer fritters to a wire rack and allow them to cool.
14. Drizzle with a glaze over the fritters.

Nutrition:
- (Per serving) Calories 391 | Fat 24g |Sodium 142mg | Carbs 38.5g | Fiber 3.5g | Sugar 21g | Protein 6.6g

Chocolate Chip Pecan Biscotti

Servings: 10
Cooking Time: 20 To 22 Minutes
Ingredients:
- 135 g finely ground blanched almond flour
- ¾ teaspoon baking powder
- ½ teaspoon xanthan gum
- ¼ teaspoon sea salt
- 3 tablespoons unsalted butter, at room temperature
- 35 g powdered sweetener
- 1 large egg, beaten
- 1 teaspoon pure vanilla extract
- 50 g chopped pecans
- 40 g organic chocolate chips,
- Melted organic chocolate chips and chopped pecans, for topping (optional)

Directions:
1. In a large bowl, combine the almond flour, baking powder, xanthan gum, and salt.
2. Line a cake pan that fits inside your air fryer with baking paper.
3. In the bowl of a stand mixer, beat together the butter and powdered sweetener. Add the beaten egg and vanilla and beat for about 3 minutes.
4. Add the almond flour mixture to the butter and egg mixture; beat until just combined.
5. Stir in the pecans and chocolate chips.
6. Transfer the dough to the prepared pan and press it into the bottom.
7. Set the air fryer to 165ºC and bake for 12 minutes. Remove from the air fryer and let cool for 15 minutes. Using a sharp knife, cut the cookie into thin strips, then return the strips to the cake pan with the bottom sides facing up.
8. Set the air fryer to 150ºC. Bake for 8 to 10 minutes.
9. Remove from the air fryer and let cool completely on a wire rack. If desired, dip one side of each biscotti piece into melted chocolate chips, and top with chopped pecans.

Fruity Blackberry Crisp

Servings: 4
Cooking Time: 15 Minutes
Ingredients:
- 2 cups blackberries
- ⅓ cup powdered erythritol
- 2 tablespoons lemon juice
- ¼ teaspoon xanthan gum
- 1 cup Crunchy Granola

Directions:
1. Mix erythritol, blackberries, xanthan gum, and lemon juice in a large bowl.
2. Place into 6&quot| round baking dish and cover with a sheet of foil. Put into the air fryer basket.
3. Set the temperature to 350ºF, then set the timer for 12 minutes.
4. When the goes off, remove the foil and shake well.
5. Sprinkle granola on the top of mixture and place back to the air fryer basket.
6. Set the temperature to 320ºF, then set the timer for 3 minutes or until the top is golden brown.
7. Serve immediately.

Cake In The Air Fryer

Servings:2
Cooking Time:30
Ingredients:
- 90 grams all-purpose flour
- Pinch of salt
- 1/2 teaspoon of baking powder
- ½ cup of tutti fruitti mix
- 2 eggs
- 1 teaspoon of vanilla extract
- 10 tablespoons of white sugar

Directions:
1. Take a bowl and add all-purpose flour, salt, and baking powder.
2. Stir it in a large bowl.
3. Whisk two eggs in a separate bowl and add vanilla extract, sugar and blend it with a hand beater.
4. Now combine wet ingredients with the dry ones.
5. Mix it well and pour it between two round pan that fits inside baskets.
6. Place the pans in both the baskets.
7. Now set the zone 1 basket to BAKE function at 310 for 30 minutes.
8. Select MATCH for zone two baskets.
9. Once it's done, serve and enjoy.

Nutrition:
- (Per serving) Calories 711| Fat4.8g| Sodium 143mg | Carbs 161g | Fiber 1.3g | Sugar 105g | Protein 10.2g

Apple Hand Pies

Servings: 8
Cooking Time: 21 Minutes.
Ingredients:
- 8 tablespoons butter, softened
- 12 tablespoons brown sugar
- 2 teaspoons cinnamon, ground
- 4 medium Granny Smith apples, diced
- 2 teaspoons cornstarch
- 4 teaspoons cold water
- 1 (14-oz) package pastry, 9-inch crust pie
- Cooking spray
- 1 tablespoon grapeseed oil
- ½ cup powdered sugar
- 2 teaspoons milk

Directions:
1. Toss apples with brown sugar, butter, and cinnamon in a suitable skillet.
2. Place the skillet over medium heat and stir cook for 5 minutes.
3. Mix cornstarch with cold water in a small bowl.
4. Add cornstarch mixture into the apple and cook for 1 minute until it thickens.
5. Remove this filling from the heat and allow it to cool.
6. Unroll the pie crust and spray on a floured surface.
7. Cut the dough into 16 equal rectangles.
8. Wet the edges of the 8 rectangles with water and divide the apple filling at the center of these rectangles.
9. Place the other 8 rectangles on top and crimp the edges with a fork, then make 2-3 slashes on top.
10. Place 4 small pies in each of the crisper plate.
11. Return the crisper plate to the Tefal Dual Zone Air Fryer.
12. Choose the Air Fry mode for Zone 1 and set the temperature to 390 degrees F and the time to 17 minutes.
13. Select the "MATCH" button to copy the settings for Zone 2.
14. Initiate cooking by pressing the START/STOP button.
15. Flip the pies once cooked halfway through, and resume cooking.
16. Meanwhile, mix sugar with milk.
17. Pour this mixture over the apple pies.
18. Serve fresh.

Nutrition:
- (Per serving) Calories 284 | Fat 16g |Sodium 252mg | Carbs 31.6g | Fiber 0.9g | Sugar 6.6g | Protein 3.7g

Victoria Sponge Cake

Servings: 8
Cooking Time: 16 Minutes
Ingredients:
- Sponge Cake Ingredients
- 400g self-rising flour
- 450g caster sugar
- 50g lemon curd
- 200g butter
- 4 medium eggs
- 1 tablespoon vanilla essence
- 480ml skimmed milk
- 1 tablespoon olive oil
- 4 tablespoons strawberry jam
- Strawberry buttercream
- 115g butter
- 210g icing sugar
- ½ teaspoon strawberry food coloring
- 1 tablespoon single cream
- 1 teaspoon vanilla essence
- 1 teaspoon maple syrup

Directions:
1. Mix sugar and butter in a bowl using a hand mixer.
2. Beat eggs with oil, and vanilla in a bowl with the mixer until creamy.
3. Stir in milk, flour and curd then mix well.
4. Add butter mixture then mix well.
5. Divide this mixture in two 4 inches greased cake pans.
6. Place one pan in each air fryer basket.
7. Return the air fryer basket 1 to Zone 1, and basket 2 to Zone 2 of the Tefal 2-Basket Air Fryer.
8. Choose the "Air Fry" mode for Zone 1 and set the temperature to 375 degrees F and 16 minutes of cooking time.
9. Select the "MATCH COOK" option to copy the settings for Zone 2.
10. Initiate cooking by pressing the START/PAUSE BUTTON.
11. Meanwhile, blend the buttercream ingredients in a mixer until fluffy.
12. Place one cake on a plate and top it with the buttercream.
13. Top it jam and then with the other cake.
14. Serve.

Nutrition:
- (Per serving) Calories 284 | Fat 16g |Sodium 252mg | Carbs 31.6g | Fiber 0.9g | Sugar 6.6g | Protein 3.7g

Monkey Bread

Servings: 12
Cooking Time: 10 Minutes
Ingredients:
- Bread
- 12 Rhodes white dinner rolls
- ½ cup brown sugar
- 1 teaspoon cinnamon
- 4 tablespoons butter melted
- Glaze
- ½ cup powdered sugar
- 1-2 tablespoons milk
- ½ teaspoon vanilla

Directions:
1. Mix brown sugar, cinnamon and butter in a bowl.
2. Cut the dinner rolls in half and dip them in the sugar mixture.
3. Place these buns in a greased baking pan and pour the remaining butter on top.
4. Place the buns in the air fryer baskets.
5. Return the air fryer basket 1 to Zone 1, and basket 2 to Zone 2 of the Tefal 2-Basket Air Fryer.
6. Choose the "Air Fry" mode for Zone 1 at 350 degrees F and 10 minutes of cooking time.
7. Initiate cooking by pressing the START/PAUSE BUTTON.
8. Flip the rolls once cooked halfway through.
9. Meanwhile, mix milk, vanilla and sugar in a bowl.
10. Pour the glaze over the air fried rolls.
11. Serve.

Nutrition:
- (Per serving) Calories 192 | Fat 9.3g |Sodium 133mg | Carbs 27.1g | Fiber 1.4g | Sugar 19g | Protein 3.2g

Lemon Sugar Cookie Bars Monster Sugar Cookie Bars

Servings:12
Cooking Time: 18 Minutes
Ingredients:
- FOR THE LEMON COOKIE BARS
- Grated zest and juice of 1 lemon
- ½ cup granulated sugar
- 4 tablespoons (½ stick) unsalted butter, at room temperature
- 1 large egg yolk
- 1 teaspoon vanilla extract
- ⅛ teaspoon baking powder
- ½ cup plus 2 tablespoons all-purpose flour
- FOR THE MONSTER COOKIE BARS
- ½ cup granulated sugar
- 4 tablespoons (½ stick) unsalted butter, at room temperature
- 1 large egg yolk
- 1 teaspoon vanilla extract
- ⅛ teaspoon baking powder
- ½ cup plus 2 tablespoons all-purpose flour
- ¼ cup rolled oats
- ¼ cup M&M's
- ¼ cup peanut butter chips

Directions:
1. To prep the lemon cookie bars: In a large bowl, rub together the lemon zest and sugar. Add the butter and use a hand mixer to beat until light and fluffy.
2. Beat in the egg yolk, vanilla, and lemon juice. Mix in the baking powder and flour.
3. To prep the monster cookie bars: In a large bowl, with a hand mixer, beat the sugar and butter until light and fluffy.
4. Beat in the egg yolk and vanilla. Mix in the baking powder and flour. Stir in the oats, M&M's, and peanut butter chips.
5. To cook the cookie bars: Line both baskets with aluminum foil. Press the lemon cookie dough into the Zone 1 basket and insert the basket in the unit. Press the monster cookie dough into the Zone 2 basket and insert the basket in the unit.
6. Select Zone 1, select BAKE, set the temperature to 330°F, and set the timer to 18 minutes. Press MATCH COOK to match Zone 2 settings to Zone 1.
7. Press START/PAUSE to begin cooking.
8. When cooking is complete, the cookies should be set in the middle and have begun to pull away from the sides of the basket.
9. Let the cookies cool completely, about 1 hour. Cut each basket into 6 bars for a total of 12 bars.

Nutrition:
- (Per serving) Calories: 191; Total fat: 8.5g; Saturated fat: 5g; Carbohydrates: 27g; Fiber: 0.5g; Protein: 2g; Sodium: 3mg

Spiced Apple Cake

Servings: 6
Cooking Time: 30 Minutes
Ingredients:
- Vegetable oil
- 2 diced & peeled Gala apples
- 1 tablespoon fresh lemon juice
- 55 g unsalted butter, softened
- 65 g granulated sugar
- 2 large eggs
- 155 g plain flour
- 1½ teaspoons baking powder
- 1 tablespoon apple pie spice
- ½ teaspoon ground ginger
- ¼ teaspoon ground cardamom
- ¼ teaspoon ground nutmeg
- ½ teaspoon kosher, or coarse sea salt
- 60 ml whole milk
- Icing sugar, for dusting

Directions:
1. Grease a 0.7-liter Bundt, or tube pan with oil; set aside.
2. In a medium bowl, toss the apples with the lemon juice until well coated; set aside.
3. In a large bowl, combine the butter and sugar. Beat with an electric hand mixer on medium speed until the sugar has dissolved. Add the eggs and beat until fluffy. Add the flour, baking powder, apple pie spice, ginger, cardamom, nutmeg, salt, and milk. Mix until the batter is thick but pourable.
4. Pour the batter into the prepared pan. Top batter evenly with the apple mixture. Place the pan in the zone 1 air fryer drawer. Set the temperature to 176°C and cook for 30 minutes, or until a toothpick inserted in the center of the cake comes out clean. Close the air fryer and let the cake rest for 10 minutes. Turn the cake out onto a wire rack and cool completely.
5. Right before serving, dust the cake with icing sugar.

Biscuit Doughnuts

Servings: 8
Cooking Time: 15 Minutes
Ingredients:
- ½ cup white sugar
- 1 teaspoon cinnamon
- ½ cup powdered sugar
- 1 can pre-made biscuit dough
- Coconut oil
- Melted butter to brush biscuits

Directions:
1. Place all the biscuits on a cutting board and cut holes in the center of each biscuit using a cookie cutter.
2. Grease the crisper plate with coconut oil.
3. Place the biscuits in the two crisper plates while keeping them 1 inch apart.
4. Return the crisper plates to the Tefal Dual Zone Air Fryer.
5. Choose the Air Fry mode for Zone 1 and set the temperature to 375 degrees F and the time to 15 minutes.
6. Select the "MATCH" button to copy the settings for Zone 2.
7. Initiate cooking by pressing the START/STOP button.
8. Brush all the donuts with melted butter and sprinkle cinnamon and sugar on top.
9. Air fry these donuts for one minute more.
10. Enjoy!

Apple Crumble

Servings: 4
Cooking Time: 30 Minutes
Ingredients:
- 1 can apple pie filling
- 6 tablespoons caster sugar
- 8 tablespoons self-rising flour
- ¼ cup butter, softened
- A pinch of salt

Directions:
1. Take a baking dish.
2. Arrange apple pie filling evenly into the prepared baking dish.
3. Take a large bowl, add all the remaining ingredients. Mix well.
4. Place the mixture evenly all over apple pie filling.
5. Press "Zone 1" and "Zone 2" and then rotate the knob for each zone to select "Bake".
6. Set the temperature to 320 degrees F/ 160 degrees C for both zones and then set the time for 5 minutes to preheat.
7. After preheating, arrange the baking dish into the basket of each zone.
8. Slide each basket into Air Fryer and set the time for 25 minutes.
9. After cooking time is completed, remove the baking dish from Air Fryer.
10. Set aside to cool.
11. Serve and enjoy!

Apple Wedges With Apricots And Coconut Mixed Berry Crisp

Servings: 10
Cooking Time: 20 Minutes
Ingredients:
- Apple Wedges with Apricots:
- 4 large apples, peeled and sliced into 8 wedges
- 2 tablespoons light olive oil
- 95 g dried apricots, chopped
- 1 to 2 tablespoons granulated sugar
- ½ teaspoon ground cinnamon
- Coconut Mixed Berry Crisp:
- 1 tablespoon butter, melted
- 340 g mixed berries
- 65 g granulated sweetener
- 1 teaspoon pure vanilla extract
- ½ teaspoon ground cinnamon
- ¼ teaspoon ground cloves
- ¼ teaspoon grated nutmeg
- 50 g coconut chips, for garnish

Directions:
1. Make the Apple Wedges with Apricots :
2. Preheat the zone 1 air fryer drawer to 180ºC.
3. Toss the apple wedges with the olive oil in a mixing bowl until well coated.
4. Place the apple wedges in the zone 1 air fryer drawer and air fry for 12 to 15 minutes.
5. Sprinkle with the dried apricots and air fry for another 3 minutes.
6. Meanwhile, thoroughly combine the sugar and cinnamon in a small bowl.
7. Remove the apple wedges from the drawer to a plate. Serve sprinkled with the sugar mixture.
8. Make the Coconut Mixed Berry Crisp :
9. Preheat the zone 2 air fryer drawer to 164ºC. Coat a baking pan with melted butter.
10. Put the remaining ingredients except the coconut chips in the prepared baking pan.
11. Bake in the preheated air fryer for 20 minutes.
12. Serve garnished with the coconut chips.

Honeyed, Roasted Apples With Walnuts & Rhubarb And Strawberry Crumble

Servings: 10
Cooking Time: 12 To 17 Minutes
Ingredients:
- Honeyed, Roasted Apples with Walnuts:
- 2 Granny Smith apples
- 20 g certified gluten-free rolled oats
- 2 tablespoons honey
- ½ teaspoon ground cinnamon
- 2 tablespoons chopped walnuts
- Pinch salt
- 1 tablespoon olive oil
- Rhubarb and Strawberry Crumble:
- 250 g sliced fresh strawberries
- 95 g sliced rhubarb
- 75 g granulated sugar
- 60 g quick-cooking oatmeal
- 50 g whole-wheat pastry flour, or plain flour
- 50 g packed light brown sugar
- ½ teaspoon ground cinnamon
- 3 tablespoons unsalted butter, melted

Directions:
1. Make the Honeyed, Roasted Apples with Walnuts :
2. Preheat the air fryer to 190ºC.
3. Core the apples and slice them in half.
4. In a medium bowl, mix together the oats, honey, cinnamon, walnuts, salt, and olive oil.
5. Scoop a quarter of the oat mixture onto the top of each half apple.
6. Place the apples in the zone 1 air fryer basket, and roast for 12 to 15 minutes, or until the apples are fork tender.
7. Make the Rhubarb and Strawberry Crumble :
8. Preheat the air fryer to 190ºC.
9. In a 6-by-2-inch round metal baking pan, combine the strawberries, rhubarb, and granulated sugar.
10. In a medium bowl, stir together the oatmeal, flour, brown sugar, and cinnamon. Stir the melted butter into this mixture until crumbly. Sprinkle the crumble mixture over the fruit.
11. Once the unit is preheated, place the pan into the zone 2 basket.
12. Bake for 12 minutes then check the crumble. If the fruit is bubbling and the topping is golden brown, it is done. If not, resume cooking.
13. When the cooking is complete, serve warm.

Simple Pineapple Sticks And Crispy Pineapple Rings

Servings: 9
Cooking Time: 10 Minutes
Ingredients:
- Simple Pineapple Sticks:
- ½ fresh pineapple, cut into sticks
- 25 g desiccated coconut
- Crispy Pineapple Rings:
- 240 ml rice milk
- 85 g plain flour
- 120 ml water
- 25 g unsweetened flaked coconut
- 4 tablespoons granulated sugar
- ½ teaspoon baking soda
- ½ teaspoon baking powder
- ½ teaspoon vanilla essence
- ½ teaspoon ground cinnamon
- ¼ teaspoon ground star anise
- Pinch of kosher, or coarse sea salt
- 1 medium pineapple, peeled and sliced

Directions:
1. Simple Pineapple Sticks :
2. Preheat the air fryer to 204°C.
3. Coat the pineapple sticks in the desiccated coconut and put in the zone 1 air fryer drawer.
4. Air fry for 10 minutes.
5. Serve immediately
6. Crispy Pineapple Rings :
7. Preheat the air fryer to 204°C.
8. In a large bowl, stir together all the ingredients except the pineapple.
9. Dip each pineapple slice into the batter until evenly coated.
10. Arrange the pineapple slices in the zone 2 drawer and air fry for 6 to 8 minutes until golden brown.
11. Remove from the drawer to a plate and cool for 5 minutes before serving warm

Apple Pie Rolls

Servings: 8
Cooking Time: 12 Minutes
Ingredients:
- 3 cups tart apples, peeled, cored and chopped
- ½ cup light brown sugar
- 2½ teaspoon ground cinnamon, divided
- 1 teaspoon corn starch
- 8 egg roll wrappers
- ½ cup cream cheese, softened
- Non-stick cooking spray
- 2 tablespoons sugar

Directions:
1. In a small bowl, mix together the apples, brown sugar, 1 teaspoon of cinnamon and corn starch.
2. Arrange 1 egg roll wrapper onto a smooth surface.
3. Spread about 1 tablespoon of cream cheese over roll, leaving 1-inch of edges.
4. Place ⅓ cup of apple mixture over one corner of a wrapper, just below the center.
5. Fold the bottom corner over filling.
6. With wet fingers, moisten the remaining wrapper edges.
7. Fold side corners toward center over the filling.
8. Roll egg roll up tightly and with your fingers, press at tip to seal.
9. Repeat with the remaining wrappers, cream cheese and filling.
10. Spray the rolls with cooking spray evenly.
11. Press "Zone 1" and "Zone 2" and then rotate the knob for each zone to select "Air Fry".
12. Set the temperature to 400 degrees F/ 200 degrees C for both zones and then set the time for 5 minutes to preheat.
13. After preheating, arrange 4 rolls into the basket of each zone.
14. Slide each basket into Air Fryer and set the time for 12 minutes.
15. While cooking, flip the rolls once halfway through and spray with the cooking spray.
16. Meanwhile, in a shallow dish, mix together the sugar and remaining cinnamon.
17. After cooking time is completed, remove the rolls from Air Fryer.
18. Coat the rolls with sugar mixture and serve.

RECIPES INDEX

A

Acorn Squash Slices 41

Air Fried Bacon And Eggs 16

Air Fried Sausage 27

Air Fryer Chicken-fried Steak 56

Air Fryer Meatloaves 48

Air Fryer Vegetables 42

Air-fried Turkey Breast With Roasted Green Bean Casserole 82

Almond Chicken 74

anadian Bacon Muffin Sandwiches And All-in-one Toast 24

Apple Crumble 97

Apple Hand Pies 95

Apple Nutmeg Flautas 93

Apple Pie Rolls 99

Apple Wedges With Apricots And Coconut Mixed Berry Crisp 98

B

Bacon & Spinach Cups 28

Bacon Cinnamon Rolls 15

Bacon Halibut Steak 65

Bacon Potato Patties 38

Bacon Wrapped Corn Cob 40

Bacon-wrapped Hot Dogs With Mayo-ketchup Sauce 55

Bacon-wrapped Shrimp 60

Bagels 27

Baked Egg And Mushroom Cups 22

Balsamic Duck Breast 73

Balsamic Steak Tips With Roasted Asparagus And Mushroom Medley 56

Banana Bread 29

Bang-bang Chicken 78

Barbecue Ribs With Roasted Green Beans And Shallots 51

Bbq Cheddar-stuffed Chicken Breasts 79

Beef And Bean Taquitos With Mexican Rice 54

Beef Skewers 33

Beefy Swiss Pastry 35

Bell Pepper Stuffed Chicken Roll-ups 76

Berry Crumble And Coconut-custard Pie 89

Biscuit Doughnuts 97

Blueberries Muffins 30

Blueberry Coffee Cake And Maple Sausage Patties 20

Blueberry Muffins 18

Bo Luc Lac 45

Breaded Scallops 71

Breakfast Calzone And Western Frittata 28

Breakfast Sammies 15

Broccoli Cheese Chicken 80

Broiled Crab Cakes With Hush Puppies 69

Brown Sugar Garlic Salmon 64

Bruschetta Chicken 83

Buffalo Bites 45

Buffalo Chicken 73

Buffalo Wings Honey-garlic Wings 30

C

Cajun Catfish Cakes With Cheese 67

Cake In The Air Fryer 94

Cauliflower Gnocchi 33

Cheddar-ham-corn Muffins 17

Cheddar-stuffed Chicken 75

Cheese Stuffed Mushrooms 32

Cheeseburgers With Barbecue Potato Chips 50

Cheesy Baked Eggs 21

Cheesy Scrambled Eggs And Egg And Bacon Muffins 24

Chicken & Veggies 83

Chicken And Potatoes 79

Chicken And Vegetable Fajitas 77

Chicken Drumettes 75

Chicken Fajitas With Street Corn 84

Chicken Legs With Leeks 79

Chicken Parmesan 72

Chicken Potatoes 72

Chicken Tenders 32

Chicken Wings With Piri Piri Sauce 83

Chicken With Bacon And Tomato & Bacon-wrapped Stuffed Chicken Breasts 84

Chickpea Fritters 43

Chili Chicken Wings 82

Chipotle Drumsticks 85

Chocolate Chip Pecan Biscotti 94

Chocolate Muffins 88

Cinnamon Bread Twists 92

Cinnamon Toast 16

Cinnamon-beef Kofta 56

Cinnamon-raisin Bagels Everything Bagels 18

Classic Fish Sticks With Tartar Sauce 61

Cod With Jalapeño 57

Coriander Lime Chicken Thighs 73

Country Prawns 59

Crispy Dill Chicken Strips 71

Crispy Hash Browns 14

Crispy Plantain Chips 32

Crispy Popcorn Shrimp 36

Croquettes 29

Crumb-topped Sole 62

Crusted Cod 66

E

Easy Breaded Pork Chops 46

Easy Mini Chocolate Chip Pan Cookie 92

Egg And Avocado In The Tefal 25

Eggs In Avocado Cups 26

F

Fajita Chicken Strips & Barbecued Chicken With Creamy Coleslaw 85

Five-ingredient Falafel With Garlic-yoghurt Sauce 36

Five-spice Pork Belly 50

Fluffy Layered Peanut Butter Cheesecake Brownies 91

Foil Packet Salmon 67

French Toast Sticks 23

Fresh Mix Veggies In Air Fryer 44

Fried Artichoke Hearts 44

Fried Avocado Tacos 40

Fried Olives 41

Fried Pickles 35

Frozen Breaded Fish Fillet 62

Fruity Blackberry Crisp 94

Fudge Brownies 92

G

Garlic Butter Steaks 47

Garlic Dill Wings 71

Garlic Potato Wedges In Air Fryer 40

Garlic-rosemary Brussels Sprouts 37

General Tso's Chicken 74

Goat Cheese And Garlic Crostini & Sweet Bacon Potato Crunchies 31

Green Tomato Stacks 43

H

Harissa-rubbed Chicken 77

Healthy Chickpea Fritters 35

Healthy Semolina Pudding 90

Healthy Spinach Balls 33

Herb Tuna Patties 64

Herbed Turkey Breast With Simple Dijon Sauce 77

Homemade Toaster Pastries 23

Honey Butter Chicken 87

Honey Sriracha Mahi Mahi 57

Honey Teriyaki Tilapia 60

Honeyed, Roasted Apples With Walnuts & Rhubarb And Strawberry Crumble 98

I

Italian Baked Cod 67

Italian Chicken & Potatoes 80

Italian Sausages With Peppers And Teriyaki Rump Steak With Broccoli 52

J

Jerk Tofu With Roasted Cabbage 38

L

Lemon Sugar Cookie Bars Monster Sugar Cookie Bars 96

Lemon Thyme Roasted Chicken 72

Lemon-blueberry Muffins 21

Lemony Prawns And Courgette 66

Lemony Sweet Twists 91

Lime Bars 90

M

Marinated Chicken Legs 86

Meatloaf 55

Mexican Breakfast Pepper Rings 22

Mini Peanut Butter Tarts 88

Mini Strawberry And Cream Pies 89

Moist Chocolate Espresso Muffins 91

Monkey Bread 96

Mozzarella Bacon Calzones 19

Mozzarella Stuffed Beef And Pork Meatballs 46

Mushroom-and-tomato Stuffed Hash Browns 16

O

Olive Oil Cake & Old-fashioned Fudge Pie 90

Orange Chicken With Roasted Snap Peas And Scallions 81

Orange-mustard Glazed Salmon And Cucumber And Salmon Salad 59

Oyster Po'boy 68

P

Panko Crusted Calf's Liver Strips 55

Paprika Pork Chops 53

Pepper Poppers 44

Pepperoni Pizza Dip 34

Perfect Cinnamon Toast 19

Perfect Parmesan Salmon 70

Pork Chops With Apples 49

Potato And Parsnip Latkes With Baked Apples 42

Potatoes & Beans 39

Prawns Curry 70

Pretzel-crusted Catfish 65

Pumpkin French Toast Casserole With Sweet And Spicy Twisted Bacon 25

Q

Quiche Breakfast Peppers 17

Quick And Easy Blueberry Muffins 20

Quickie Cinnamon Sugar Pork Rinds 89

R

Ravioli 34

Roast Souvlaki-style Pork With Lemon-feta Baby Potatoes 53

Roasted Halibut Steaks With Parsley 68

Roasted Oranges 22

Roasted Salmon And Parmesan Asparagus 63

Rosemary Asparagus & Potatoes 37

S

Salmon Nuggets 64

Salmon Patties 58

Salmon With Cauliflower 57

Salmon With Fennel Salad 62

Sausage And Cheese Balls 22

Sausage And Egg Breakfast Burrito 27

Sausage And Pork Meatballs 48

Sausage Meatballs 47

Sausage With Eggs 17

Scallops 68

Seasoned Flank Steak 51

Sesame Honey Salmon 66

Shrimp Pirogues 34

Shrimp With Lemon And Pepper 70

Simple Beef Sirloin Roast 49

Simple Pineapple Sticks And Crispy Pineapple Rings 99

Smoked Salmon 61

Soft Pecan Brownies 87

Sole And Cauliflower Fritters And Prawn Bake 65

Spiced Apple Cake 97

Spice-rubbed Chicken Pieces 78

Spicy Chicken Sandwiches With "fried" Pickles 86

Spinach Patties 36

Steak And Mashed Creamy Potatoes 47

Steak Fajitas With Onions And Peppers 46

Stuffed Apples 87

Stuffed Mushrooms With Crab 57

Stuffed Sweet Potatoes 41

Stuffed Tomatoes 37

Sweet And Spicy Carrots With Chicken Thighs 78

Sweet Potato Hash 22

Sweet Potato Sausage Hash 14

T

Tangy Fried Pickle Spears 31

Tasty Lamb Patties 52

Tasty Pork Skewers 48

Tender Pork Chops 51

Thai Curry Chicken Kabobs 81

Tilapia Sandwiches With Tartar Sauce 58

Tomahawk Steak 49

Tuna Patties 69

Tuna Patties With Spicy Sriracha Sauce Coconut Prawns 63

Tuna Steaks 61

Tuna With Herbs 60

Turkey And Beef Meatballs 54

Turkey And Cranberry Quesadillas 76

Turkey Ham Muffins 26

Turkey Meatloaf With Veggie Medley 76

V

Vanilla Strawberry Doughnuts 26

Veggie Burgers With "fried" Onion Rings 39

Victoria Sponge Cake 95

W

Waffle Fries 31

Walnuts Fritters 93

Wholemeal Blueberry Muffins 21

Wings With Corn On Cob 75

Y

Yellow Potatoes With Eggs 19

Yummy Chicken Breasts 80

Printed in Great Britain
by Amazon